This book is a great tool a toolbox. I've used many boc by far the most user friendly. The addition of geographical information makes this book especially wonderful, as combining the geographical information together gives new and improved understanding of the context of many of Jesus' sermons and parables. The information is laid out in very easily understood tables that will make studying out common threads through the Gospels much easier. This reference book will be coming off the bookshelf on a regular basis, I can promise that.
**Pastor Tom Otto**

This book is a result of much careful study of the Gospel Records and is evidence that the author loves to study God's Word. He answers many questions that most Bible students have had about geography and the harmony of the accounts of our Lord's ministry. I really enjoyed the charts and notes that synthesized the events surrounding the death and resurrection of Jesus. This book is an excellent resource for all students of the Bible.
**Pastor Jamin Boyer**

This short volume is packed full of helpful charts and list. The research and study involved in this work are a credit to the author and his team. This is solid choice for any serious student of the life of Christ.
**Pastor Mike Montgomery**

Jimmy Reagan has done a wonderful job of compiling a great deal of information in a very concise format. The charts make this volume extremely useful. I believe it will serve as a good quick reference for those who are serious about studying the life of Christ.
**Dr. Scott Pauley**

Pastor Reagan is one of the most well-read ministers that I have ever been around. For many years in my own ministry I have gleaned from his wisdom and study. *Following Jesus through the Gospels* is a culmination of years of study on the life of Christ. In this valuable book, he harmonizes the events of the Gospel records and presents the information in usable chart form. You can now see various aspects of the Gospel records on one page at a time. This is treasure for any student of God's Word and a handy resource for all preachers.
**Pastor Mark Fowler**

This book will prove to be most helpful for anyone studying through the life of Christ. It is loaded with information that is able to be both quickly accessible and easily understood. You will find it more study guide than book, but its affordable price and handy size, make it a great companion to scripture while reading through the gospels.
**Pastor Allen Gibson**

Pastor Reagan shows the ability to simplify the most challenging of topics in this chart filled book. There is no more vital topic for understanding than the life of Jesus Christ! I remember when the topics were first taught and put into chart form; they helped me and they will help you.
**Pastor Ryan Brown**

# Following Jesus Through the Gospels

*Making Sense of the Chronological and Geographic Details Along with the Teaching Methods of Jesus*

Jimmy R. Reagan

Copyright © 2016 Jimmy R. Reagan

All rights reserved. No part of this book may be reproduced, stored in a retrieval system, or transmitted in any form or by any means—electronic, mechanical, photocopy, recording, or otherwise—without written permission of the author, except for brief quotations in printed reviews.

ISBN: 978-1540559623

# Chart Guide

Brief Overview Harmony / 5
Incarnation, Birth and Youth / 8
Baptism and Temptation / 10
Galilee, Judea, and Samaria Ministry / 12
Early Great Ministry in Galilee / 14
Late Great Ministry in Galilee / 16
Last Ministry in Perea and Judea / 18
Last Days in Jerusalem / 20
Harmony of the Gospels / 22
Statistics of the Gospels / 35
Recorded Parables of Jesus Christ / 37
Recorded Miracles of Jesus Christ / 38
Public Sermons of Jesus Christ / 41
Personal Discourses of Jesus Christ / 43
Personal Encounters of Jesus Christ / 45
The Cries of Christ on the Cross / 47
The Post-Resurrection Appearances of Jesus Christ / 48
Synthesis of the Birth and Infancy of Jesus Christ / 51
Synthesis of the Upper Room and Gethseman / 53
Synthesis of the Trial of Jesus Christ / 55
Synthesis of the Day of Crucufixion / 57
Synthesis of the Events from the Resurrection to the Ascension / 59

# Preface

Jesus. Can we ever take in all He means to us? The Gospels. Can we ever find more fruitful fields to know Him Whom we love? The Gospels are a glistening prism that provides everything from panoramic vistas to close-up portraits of Christ.

Because the four Gospels of Matthew Mark, Luke, and John do such a masterful job in sharing their respective theme of Jesus Christ as designed by the Spirit of God, we who study God's Word have the challenge of tying them together as a whole for a composite picture. We don't deny that the way they are given to us is best, but we surely see the value of digging out a unified portrait as well.

Over a decade ago, Ryan Brown, pastor of Calvary Baptist Church in Portsmouth, Ohio, asked me to teach on the Gospels in his School of the Bible. My love affair with the Gospels has only continued to grow in the intervening years. While I hope to write more on the Gospels someday, I have become convinced that we need something of a manageable size to tag along with our Bibles to help us make sense of chronology, geography, and the unique teaching tools Jesus used in His earthly ministry.

I love Jesus. Sadly, that statement has become rather cliché in our jaded age, but this simple believer still means it with all his heart. If this booklet helps a sincere Bible student come to see Jesus a little more vividly through His Gospels, I will be amply rewarded.

*Thanksgiving 2016*

# Following Jesus Through the Gospels

*Making Sense of the Chronological and Geographic Details Along with The Pedagogical Methods of Jesus*

## Time and Place

One of the things that the casual reader of the Gospels often misses is the issue of time and place of the event on the page. Though there are numerous chronological and geographic details given in the Gospels, there's often not enough detail in the passage at hand alone to place the event in Christ's earthly ministry. There are, however, enough details across the Gospels together to make sense of it. The fact of these details coupled with their apparent elusiveness is the reason for this booklet—to do that organizing work for you to enrich your reading of these four treasures known collectively as the Gospels.

To gain the most from this chronological and geographic information, you would do well to think in terms of the general stages of Jesus' ministry. You will notice when you do that there are differing geographic emphases in most every stage. Here is a chart to orient you to these chronological and geographic details given in the Gospels.

**NOTE TO READERS:**

The charts in this volume are based on my belief that the Crucifixion took place on Wednesday with Thursday being the High Sabbath of Passover. Many Bible students believe Thursday is the correct day of the Crucifixion. The most commonly believed day is Friday, though I find it highly implausible to fit three days AND three nights into that timeframe. Though Jewish people often counted part of a day as a whole, the Bible emphasizing three days and nights suggests at least 72 hours was in view.

Still, these charts can be adjusted to either of the other models by making either Wednesday or Wednesday and Thursday as silent days in Scripture. With that change, the charts will still work for your studies.

## Figure 1: Brief Overview Harmony

### A Brief Overview Harmony of the Gospels

| Stage of Ministry | Matthew | Mark | Luke | John |
|---|---|---|---|---|
| The Incarnation | | | | 1:1-18 |
| Birth and Youth | 1:1-2:23 | | 1:1-2:38 | |
| Beginning of Ministry, Baptism & Temptation | 3:1-4:11 | 1:1-13 | 3:1-4:13 | 1:19-34 |
| Early Ministry in Galilee, Judea & Samaria | | | | 1:35-4:42 |
| Early Great Ministry in Galilee | 4:12-14:12 | 1:14-6:29 | 4:14-9:9 | 4:43-5:47 |
| Late Great Ministry in Galilee | 14:13-18:35 | 6:30-9:50 | 9:10-9:50 | 6:1-7:10 |
| Last Ministry in Perea and Judea | 19:1-20:34 | 10:1-10:52 | 9:51-19:27 | 7:11-12:11 |
| **Last Days In Jerusalem*** | | | | |
| Saturday ~ *Triumphal Entry*  *Nisan 9* | 21:1-11 | 11:1-11 | 19:28-44 | 12:12-19 |
| Sunday ~ *Curses Fig Tree & Cleanses Temple*  *Nisan 10* | 21:12-19 | 11:12-19 | 19:45-48 | |
| Monday ~ *Sees Cursed Fig Tree*  ~ *Encountering Sadducees & Pharisees*  ~ *Teaches*  *Nisan 11* | 21:20-26:5 | 11:20-14:2 | 20:1-22:2 | 12:20-50 |
| Tuesday ~ *Lord's Supper*  ~ *Judas Plans Betrayal*  ~ *Gethsemane*  ~ *The Arrest*  ~ *First of Religious Trials*  *Nisan 12* | 26:6-75 | 14:3-72 | 22:3-65 | 13:1-18:27 |
| Wednesday ~ *Last of Religious & Civil Trials*  ~ *Crucifixion*  ~ *Burial*  *Nisan 13* | 27:1-61 | 15:1-46 | 22:66-23:54 | 18:28-19:42 |
| Thursday ~ *In Grave*  ~ *Tomb Sealed*  *Nisan 14* | 27:62-66 | | 23:55-56 | |
| Friday ~ *In Grave*  *Nisan 15* | | | | |
| Saturday ~ *In Grave*  ~ *Women Watched*  *Nisan 16* | | 15:47 | | |
| Sunday ~ *Resurrection*  *Nisan 17* | 28:1-15 | 16:1-14 | 24:1-43 | 20:1-25 |
| 40 Days & Ascension | 28:16-20 | 16:15-20 | 24:44-53 | 20:26-21:25 |

*\* Days reckoned by modern standards and not by the old Jewish designation.*

# Notes

As you see, there are eight stages of Jesus' ministry. The next thing you will likely notice is that the stage "Last Days in Jerusalem" takes up a third or more of each Gospel. That means several chapters of each Gospel are only about one week of Jesus' ministry. It is, of course, the most important week in history, but it is still just one week of His three-and-one-half year ministry.

You also see that the Gospels are not a typical biography that attempts to cover the whole of the subject's life. Matthew and Luke give us two chapters each up through His youth, John in a unique way part of one, and Mark no chapters at all. None of the Gospels tell us anything of His life from ages twelve to thirty. Clearly, the Gospels are highly selective in what is chosen to be shared. The bulk of each Gospel record, then, analyzes intensely His earthly ministry. Each Gospel further lingers over the week of the Crucifixion. That week, as you know, gets this coverage for its central significance to the message of the entire Bible.

As you begin to analyze the time periods of the life and ministry of Jesus, you will notice the time of the Incarnation, birth, and youth Christ.

## Figure 2: The Incarnation, Birth and Youth

# The Ministry of Jesus Christ

## The Incarnation, Birth and Youth of Jesus Christ
*(Mt. 1:1-2:23; Lk. 1:1-2:38; Jn. 1:1-18)*

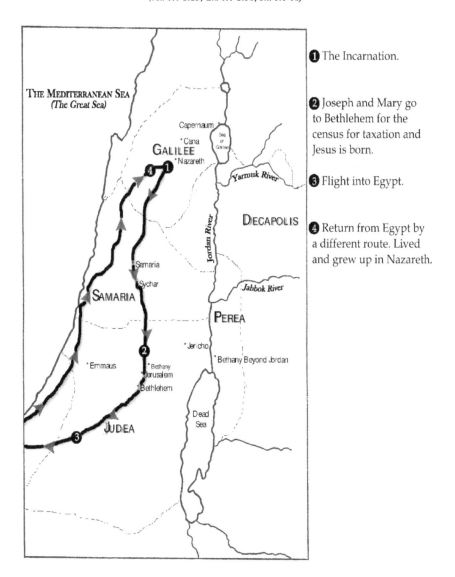

❶ The Incarnation.

❷ Joseph and Mary go to Bethlehem for the census for taxation and Jesus is born.

❸ Flight into Egypt.

❹ Return from Egypt by a different route. Lived and grew up in Nazareth.

After you get past the minimal coverage of the stage "Incarnation, Birth, and Youth" of Christ, you see the other six stages cover His brief earthly ministry. The stage "Beginning of Ministry, Baptism, and Temptation" gets some coverage in all four Gospels. This stage is the setting up, or sending forth if you will, of His ministry. Notice that there really is no geographic trend in this season of His ministry.

**Figure 3: Baptism and Temptation**

# The Ministry of Jesus Christ
## Beginning of Ministry, Baptism and Temptation
*(Mt. 3:1 4:11; Mk. 1:1-13; Lk. 3:1-4:13; Jn. 1:19-34)*

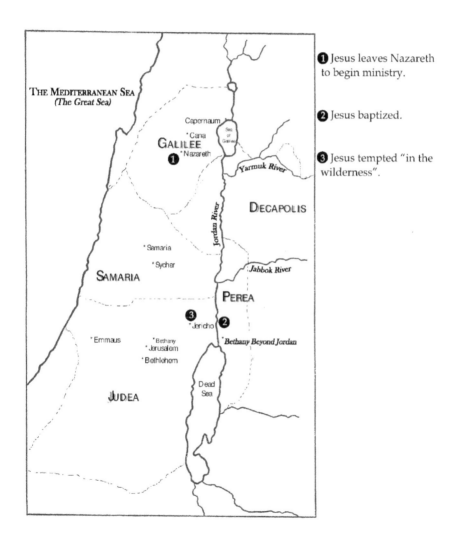

The next stage is the "Early Ministry in Galilee, Judea, and Samaria." The unique feature of this stage is that only John's Gospel records the events of this period. At this point, there is still no geographical trend present. There were several "firsts" in this epoch of ministry—first miracle, first trip to Capernaum His future ministry headquarters, first trip to Jerusalem during His ministry, and the first cleansing of the Temple.

**Figure 4: Galilee, Judea, and Samaria Ministry**

# The Ministry of Jesus Christ
## In Galilee, Judea and Samaria
*(John 1:35-4:42)*

1. Jesus first miracle - Turning water into wine.

2. Went to Capernaum for first time.

3. First trip to Jerusalem during ministry. Cleansed Temple for first time. Tells Nicodemus about being "born again".

4. Returns to Galilee briefly then goes to Samaria and meets the woman at the well. Then returns to Galilee again.

5. Heals Nobleman's Son in Cana.

6. While in Jerusalem for Passover He heals the Impotent Man.

The next stage of ministry called here "Early Great Ministry in Galilee" begins the first half of the extraordinary ministry that has always thrilled Bible readers. In this portion of His ministry He mostly ministered in Galilee among the common people. The most peculiar feature of this period is that it is the only one where the Gospel of Matthew leaves reporting chronologically and instead reports the material thematically. The chart below shows the great highlights of this period.

## Figure 5: Early Great Ministry in Galilee

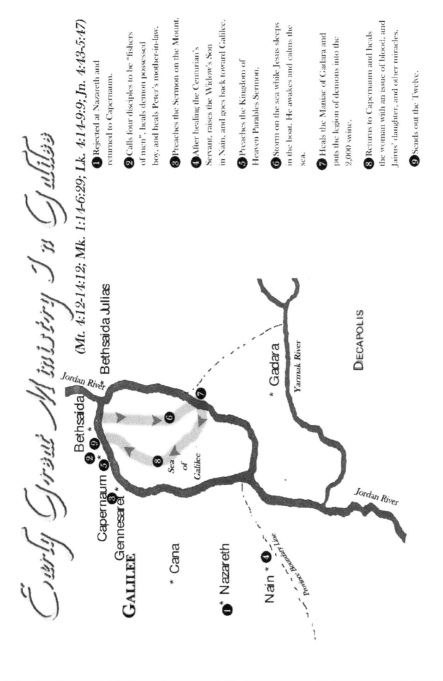

The next phase is the "Late Great Ministry in Galilee." The thrills continue in Galilee as more amazing miracles take place. If you compare the previous and following maps, you will see that the sending out of the Twelve is the natural division for the Great Galilean Ministry. The aspect that is most notably different in this later period is the growing hostility toward Christ and His ministry. You will also notice that He went outside the borders of Israel, north of Galilee, a few times in this period. For the most obvious reason to distinguish from the earlier ministry period, Matthew's Gospel returns to a chronological approach in this phase.

# Figure 6: Late Great Ministry in Galilee

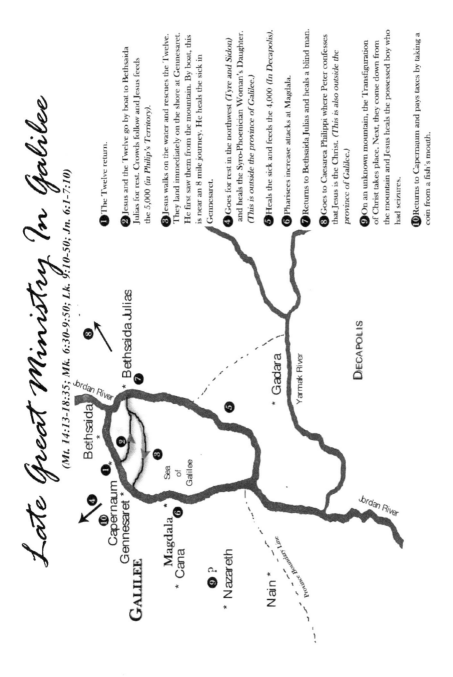

In the next section, "Last Ministry in Perea and Judea," Jesus leaves Galilee and has a clear geographical emphasis in Perea and Judea. Perea is along the route that pilgrims traveled from Galilee to Jerusalem. The key to this ministry period is that it becomes the last journey of Jesus to Jerusalem. Actually, this trip was the journey to go to die on the Cross! Along this path, He ministers every step of the way. Luke's Gospel, by far, gets the task of relating this period to us.

# Figure 7: Last Ministry in Perea and Judea

## *The Ministry of Jesus Christ*
### In Perea and Toward Jerusalem
*(Mt. 19:1-20:34; Mk. 10:1-10:52; Lk. 9:51-19:27; Jn. 7:11-12:11)*

❶ Leaves Galilee

❷ Goes to an unknown village in Samaria and is rejected.

❸ Goes on to Jerusalem for the Feast of Booths and stops for various other events.

❹ Goes back to the top of Perea (out of the districts of Galilee or Judea) where opposition is less. Works in this area for a few months.

❺ Goes for a brief visit back to Bethany to raise Lazarus, then heads back to Perea.

❻ Goes briefly into Samaria and Galilee. Leaves Galilee for the last time before His death and Resurrection.

❼ Takes slow last journey to Jerusalem with the multitude going for Passover. Teaches and preaches along the way.

❽ Crosses the Jordan River and goes through Jericho and ascends to Jerusalem for His great sacrifice.

*ARROW IS THE LAST JOURNEY OF JESUS.*

The final section, "The Last Days in Jerusalem", is that incredible time where each of the Gospels slow down to admire Jesus in His greatest act of ministry—dying for our sins.

## Figure 8: The Last Days in Jerusalem

# The Ministry of Jesus Christ
## Jerusalem ~ The Scene of the Death, Burial and Resurrection
*(Mt. 21:1-28:20; Mk. 11:1-16:20; Lk. 19:28-24:53; Jn. 12:12-21:25)*

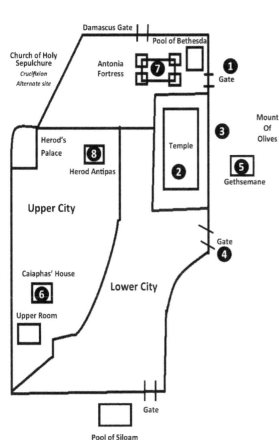

1. On Saturday, Jesus makes His triumphal entry and then goes back out of the city.

2. On Sunday before the Crucifixion, Jesus re-enters Jerusalem by the same route as #1 and cleanses the Temple and then leaves.

3. Jesus enters Jerusalem again by either #1 or #4 and encounters Sadducees and Pharisees.

4. On Tuesday, Jesus enters Jerusalem by the lower city and goes to the Upper Room.

5. Later that evening, He goes to Gethsemane teaching as He goes and praying His High Priestly prayer (Jn. 17) before arriving. He goes through His terrors there.

6. Jesus is arrested and goes to Caiaphas' house (stopping by Annas' house) for His religious trials.

7. At daybreak Wednesday, Jesus is taken to Pilate for His civil trials.

8. Pilate sends Jesus to Herod Antipas who mocks Jesus, and send Him back by the same route.

9. At the end of His trial, Jesus is taken to Golgotha (Calvary) and His crucifixion begins by 9:00 a.m. At 3:00 p.m. Jesus dies.

10. Near dusk, Jesus is taken to His tomb. By Sunday morning, He has resurrected.

## Harmony of the Gospels

Now that we have some idea of the design of the Gospels in presenting the life and ministry of Christ along with the stages of His ministry, we are in a better position to use a Harmony of the Gospels to our advantage. This Harmony of the Gospels retains the stages of Christ's ministry and puts every verse of the Gospels in its chronological order and setting. As you study this Harmony, be sure to read the guide that explains how to use this Harmony in the first paragraph of the Notes that follow.

# Figure 9: Harmony of the Gospels and Notes

## HARMONY OF THE GOSPELS

| EVENT | PLACE | MT | MK | LK | JN |
|---|---|---|---|---|---|
| **The Incarnation (From Eternity Into Time)** | | | | | |
| 1. The Incarnation ~ (Introduction of John) | Heaven to Earth | | | | 1:1-8 |
| **Birth and Youth (6 B.C. - 8 A.D.)** | | | | | |
| 2. Jesus Christ's Kingly Credentials ~ (Introduction of Matthew) | ——— | 1:1-17 | | | |
| 3. The Divine Inspiration of the Gospels ~ (Introduction of Luke) | ——— | | | 1:1-4 | |
| 4. Gabriel Appears To Zacharias Announcing the Forerunner (John the Baptist) | Jerusalem (Temple) | | | 1:5-25 | |
| 5. Gabriel Appears To Mary Announcing the Virgin Birth of Jesus | Nazareth | | | 1:26-38 | |
| 6. Mary Visits Elizabeth and Elizabeth Gives Song To Mary | City of Judea in Hill Country | | | 1:39-45 | |
| 7. Mary Gives Song of Praise and After 3 Months Mary Goes Home | City of Judea in Hill Country | | | 1:46-56 | |
| 8. Birth of John the Baptist and Zacharias' Praise | City of Judea in Hill Country | | | 1:57-80 | |
| 9. An Angel Appears To Joseph Announcing the Virgin Conception of Jesus Christ in Mary, His Espoused | City of Judea in Hill Country | 1:18-25 | | | |
| 10. Mary and Joseph Travel To Bethlehem | Nazareth to Bethlehem | | | 2:1-5 | |
| 11. The Virgin Birth of Christ | Bethlehem | 1:25 | | 2:6-7 | |
| 12. An Angel Appears To the Shepherds | In the Fields of Bethelehem | | | 2:8-12 | |
| 13. Heavenly Host Praise God | Heavens Above Bethlehem | | | 2:13-14 | |
| 14. The Shepherds Visit Baby Jesus | Bethlehem | | | 2:15-20 | |
| 15. Jesus Is Circumcised | Bethlehem | | | 2:21 | |
| 16. Jesus Is Presented As Firstborn In Temple | Jerusalem | | | 2:22-24 | |
| 17. Simeon Rejoices Over Jesus | Jerusalem | | | 2:25-35 | |
| 18. Anna Praises God For Jesus & They Return To Bethlehem | Jerusalem | | | 2:36-38 | |
| 19. The Visit Of the Wise Men | Jerusalem & Bethlehem | 2:1-12 | | | |
| 20. The Flight Into Egypt and Slaughter of Infants | Bethlehem To Egypt | 2:13-18 | | | |
| 21. The Return From Egypt | Egypt To Nazareth | 2:19-23 | | | |
| 22. The Childhood of Jesus and Visit To Jerusalem At Age 12 | Nazareth & Jerusalem | | | 2:39-52 | |

| EVENT | PLACE | MT | MK | LK | JN |
|---|---|---|---|---|---|
| **Beginning of Ministry, Baptism & Temptation (26-27 A.D.)** | | | | | |
| 23. Has His Forerunner (John the Baptist) Prepare the Way | Judean Wilderness and Jordan River | 3:1-12 | 1:1-8 | 3:1-20 | |
| 24. Launches Ministry As He Is Baptized | Jordan River | 3:13-17 | 1:9-11 | 3:21-22 | |
| 25. Has His Credentials Given As the Son of Man | — | | | 3:23-38 | |
| 26. Fasts For 40 Days and Faces Temptation In the Wilderness | Judean Wilderness | 4:1-11 | 1:12,13 | 4:1-13 | |
| 27. Has John Testify To Sanhedrin Members Of Who He Is | Bethany beyond Jordan | | | | 1:19-28 |
| 28. Returns To John and Has John Declare Him As the Lamb of God | Bethany beyond Jordan | | | | 1:29-34 |
| **Early Ministry In Galilee, Judea and Samaria (27 A.D.)** | | | | | |
| 29. Saves First Of What Will Become the 12 Disciples | Galilee | | | | 1:35-51 |
| 30. Turns Water Into Wine At A Wedding *(M #1) (PE #1)* | Cana | | | | 2:1-11 |
| 31. Makes First Visit To Capernaum | Capernaum | | | | 2:12 |
| 32. Goes To Jerusalem and Cleanses Temple For the First Time [*First Passover*] | Galilee to Jerusalem | | | | 2:13-22 |
| 33. Experiences Warm Acceptance In Jerusalem | Jerusalem | | | | 2:23-25 |
| 34. Teaches Nicodemus About Being Born Again (PE #2) | Jerusalem | | | | 3:1-21 |
| 35. Co-labors With His Forerunner (John the Baptist) | Judea | | | | 3:22-30 |
| 36. Meets Woman At the Well and Many Believe | Sychar in Samaria | | | | 4:1-42 |
| **Early Great Ministry In Galilee (27 A.D. [Fall] - 29 A.D. [Spring])** | | | | | |
| 37. Begins Great Galilee Ministry | Galilee | 4:12 | 1:14-15 | 4:14-15 | 4:43-45 |
| 38. Heals the Nobleman's Son (M #2) | Cana | | | | 4:46-54 |
| 39. Is Rejected In Nazareth (M #3) (S #1) | Nazareth | 4:13a | | 4:16-30 | |
| 40. Moves To Capernaum And Preaches | Capernaum | 4:13b-17 | | | |
| 41. Calls First Disciples To The Ministry | Shore of Galilee near Capernaum | 4:18-22 | 1:16-20 | | |
| 42. Heals A Demon Possessed Man and Teaches (M #4) (PD #1) | Capernaum | | 1:21-28 | 4:31-37 | |
| 43. Heals Peter's Mother-In-Law (M #5) | Capernaum | 8:14-15 | 1:29-31 | 4:38-40a | |
| 44. Heals Many Sick One Evening (M #6) | Capernaum | 8:16-17 | 1:32-34 | 4:40b-41 | |
| 45. Goes On First Preaching Tour Of Galilee | Galilee | 4:23-25 | 1:35-39 | 4:42-44 | |
| 46. Catches First Draught Of Fishes (M #7) | Sea of Galilee near Capernaum | | | 5:1-11 | |

| EVENT | PLACE | MT | MK | LK | JN |
|---|---|---|---|---|---|
| 47. Cleanses A Leper (M #8) | A Galilean Town | 8:2-4 | 1:40-45 | 5:12-16 | |
| 48. Heals A Man With Palsy (M #9) | Capernaum | 9:1-8 | 2:1-12 | 5:17-26 | |
| 49. Calls Matthew | Capernaum | 9:9-13 | 2:13-17 | 5:27-32 | |
| 50. Faces Confrontation Over Fasting (P #1) | Capernaum | 9:14-17 | 2:18-22 | 5:33-39 | |
| 51. Goes For Second Passover And Heals Impotent Man And Preaches (M #10) (S #2) [Second Passover] | Jerusalem | | | | 5:1-47 |
| 52. Faces Confrontation Over Picking Grain On The Sabbath | Near Galilee | 12:1-8 | 2:23-28 | 6:1-5 | |
| 53. Heals Man With Withered Hand In Ongoing Battle With The Pharisees (M #11) | Galilee | 12:9-14 | 3:1-6 | 6:6-11 | |
| 54. Heals Many In A Multitude (M #12) | Near Sea of Galilee | 12:15-21 | 3:7-12 | | |
| 55. Selects Twelve Apostles After Night Of Prayer | Near Capernaum | | 3:13-19 | 6:12-16 | |
| 56. Preaches The Sermon On The Mount (S #3) (P # 2) | A mountain near Capernaum | 5:1-8:1 | | 6:17-49 | |
| 57. Heals The Centurion's Servant (M #13) | Capernaum | 8:5-13 | | 7:1-10 | |
| 58. Raises A Widow's Son (M #14) | Nain | | | 7:11-17 | |
| 59. Addresses John's Doubts And His Character To The People And Preaches (S # 4) | Galilee | 11:2-19 | | 7:18-35 | |
| 60. Pronounces Woe On Chorazin, Bethsaida and Capernaum Couples With A Grand Invitation | Galilee | 11:20-30 | | | |
| 61. Accepts Anointing By A Sinful Woman (P #3) | At Simon the Pharisee's house in Capernaum | | | 7:36-50 | |
| 62. Goes On Second Tour Of Galilee With Some Godly Women Following | Galilee | | | 8:1-3 | |
| 63. Faces Charge Of Blasphemy With Scribes And Pharisees Demanding A Sign And Preaches (S # 5) | Capernaum | 12:22-45 | 3:20-30 | | |
| 64. Preaches His Kingdom of Heaven Parable Sermon With An Interruption By His Mother And Brethren. (P #4-12) (S # 6) | By Sea of Galilee In Capernaum | 12:46-13:52 | 3:31-4:34 | 8:4-21 | |
| 65. Sends Disciples Ahead Onto The Sea of Galilee And Encourages A Scribe And Another Follower To Full Surrender | Near Shore of Galilee | 8:19-22 | | | |
| 66. Calms The Storm (M #15) | Sea of Galilee | 8:23-27 | 4:35-41 | 8:22-25 | |
| 67. Heals The Maniac of Gadara (M #16) | Eastern Shore of Galilee | 8:28-34 | 5:1-10 | 8:26-39 | |
| 68. Heals The Woman With An Issue Of Blood and Jairus' Daughter (M #17-18) | Capernaum | 9:18-26 | 5:21-43 | 8:40-56 | |
| 69. Heals The Two Blind Men (M # 19) | Galilee | 9:27-31 | | | |
| 70. Heals The Demon Possessed Mute Man (M # 20) | Galilee | 9:32-34 | | | |
| 71. Makes Final Trip To Nazareth And Is Rejected Again | Nazareth | 13:53-58 | 6:1-6 | | |
| 72. Sends The Twelve Forth After Teaching And Has Third Tour Of Galilee (PD #2) | Galilee | 9:35-11:1 | 6:6-13 | 9:1-6 | |
| 73. Hears Report Of Herod Beheading John The Baptist | Galilee | 14:1-12 | 6:14-29 | 9:7-9 | |

| EVENT | PLACE | MT | MK | LK | JN |
|---|---|---|---|---|---|
| **Late Great Ministry In Galilee (29 A.D. [Spring] - October)** | | | | | |
| 74. Has The Twelve Return | Galilee, Perhaps Near Capernaum | | 6:30 | 9:10 | |
| 75. Feeds The 5,000 (M #21) [*Third Passover*] | Bethsaida Julius | 14:13-21 | 6:31-44 | 9:11-17 | 6:1-14 |
| 76. Walks On The Sea And Stops The Storm (M #22) | Sea of Galilee | 14:22-33 | 6:45-52 | | 6:15-21 |
| 77. Heals Many At Gennesaret (M #23) | Gennesaret | 14:34-36 | 6:53-56 | | |
| 78. Preaches Bread of Life Sermon To Crowd Returning From Bethsaida Julius And Many Leave (*Galilee Rejects*) (S #7) | Capernaum | | | | 6:22-7:1 |
| 79. Faces The Pharisees of Jerusalem Who Came To Galilee And Preaches (S #8) | Probably Capernaum | 15:1-20 | 7:1-23 | | |
| 80. Leaves For Rest In Tyre And Sidon And Heals The Syro-Phonecian Woman's Daughter (M #24) | Phoenicia | 15:21-28 | 7:24-30 | | |
| 81. Makes Another Journey Outside Of Galilee And Heals The Deaf And Mute Man (M #25) | Decapolis | | 7:31-37 | | |
| 82. Heals Others At Decapolis (M #26) | Decapolis | 15:29-31 | | | |
| 83. Feeds The 4000 (M #27) | Decapolis | 15:32-38a | 8:1-10a | | |
| 84. Faces Increasing Attack Of the Pharisees | Magdala | 15:38b-16:4 | 8:10b-12 | | |
| 85. Lectures Disciples On Boat To Bethsaida Julius | Sea of Galilee | 16:5-12 | 8:13-21 | | |
| 86. Heals Blind Man (M #28) | Bethsaida Julius | | 8:22-26 | | |
| 87. Tests Faith Of The Twelve And Peter Makes Great Confession | Near Caesarea Philippi | 16:13-20 | 8:27-30 | 9:18-21 | |
| 88. Foretells His Death Clearly And Teaches The Twelve (PD #3) | Near Caesarea Philippi | 16:21-28 | 8:31-9:1 | 9:22-27 | |
| 89. Transfigures On The Mountain Before Peter, James And John (M #29) | Unnamed mountain (probably in Galilee) | 17:1-13 | 9:2-13 | 9:28-36 | |
| 90. Heals The Possessed Boy Who Had Seizures (M #30) | Near the unnamed mountain (probably in Galilee) | 17:14-21 | 9:14-29 | 9:37-43a | |
| 91. Moves Quietly In Galilee And Again Foretells His Death And Resurrection | Galilee | 17:22-23 | 9:30-32 | 9:43b-45 | |
| 92. Gets A Coin In A Fishes Mouth For Taxes (M #31) | Capernaum | 17:24-27 | | | |
| 93. Teaches The Twelve In The First Who-Is-The-Greatest Discourse (PD #4) And Addresses Some Others On Full Surrender (P #13) | Capernaum | 18:1-35 | 9:33-50 | 9:46-50 | |
| 94. Rejects His Brethren's Advice | Galilee | | | | 7:2-9 |
| 95. Leaves Galilee | Galilee to Samaria | | | | 7:10 |
| **Last Ministry In Judea And Perea (29 A.D. [October] - 30 A.D. [Spring])** | | | | | |
| 96. After Leaving Galilee He Goes Through Samaria (*Samaria Rejects*) | Samaria | | | 9:51-56 | |
| 97. Addresses Others For The Third Time On Need Of Full Surrender (PE #3) | From Samaria to Judea | | | 9:57-62 | |
| 98. Arrives In Jerusalem For The Feast Of Booths And Preaches The Living Water Sermon (S #9) | Jerusalem | | | | 7:11-53 |

| EVENT | PLACE | MT | MK | LK | JN |
|---|---|---|---|---|---|
| 99. Begins Preaching The "I AM" Sermon (S #10) And Helps The Woman In Adultery (PE # 4) | Jerusalem (near Temple) | | | | 8:1-11 |
| 100. Continues Preaching With Many Interruptions By The Pharisees Who Try To Kill him, But He Vanishes (M #32) | Jerusalem (near Temple) | | | | 8:12-59 |
| 101. Heals A Man Born Blind (M #33) And Battles Pharisees | Jerusalem | | | | 9:1-38 |
| 102. Preaches The Good Shepherd Sermon (S #11) | Jerusalem | | | | 9:39-10:31 |
| 103. Sends Out The Seventy And Preaches The Christian Worker's Sermon (S #12) | Judea | | | 10:1-24 | |
| 104. Answers Question Of An Insincere Lawyer With The Parable Of The Good Samaritan (P #14) | Judea | | | 10:25-37 | |
| 105. Visits Martha And Mary And Teaches Them | Bethany | | | 10:38-42 | |
| 106. Teaches The Disciples With The Prayer Discourse (PD #5) And The Parable Of The Persistent Friend (P #15) | Judea | | | 11:1-13 | |
| 107. Casts Out A Demon (M #34) And Answers To The Charge Of Blasphemy | Judea | | | 11:14-36 | |
| 108. Dines With A Pharisee And Describes Their Folly To No Response | Judea | | | 11:37-54 | |
| 109. Preaches Sermon On The Plain (S #13) Containing The Parable Of The Rich Fool And Of The Faithful Servant (P #16,17) | Judea | | | 12:1-59 | |
| 110. Explains Two Current Events In Demanding Repentance And Gives The Parable Of The Barren Fig Tree (P #18) | Judea | | | 13:1-9 | |
| 111. Heals The Infirm Bent-Over Woman (M #35) And Repeats The Parable Of The Mustard Seed And Of The Leaven (P #6,7 repeated) | Perea or Judea | | | 13:10-21 | |
| 112. Goes To The Feast Of Dedication And The Jews Question Him On Being The Christ | Jerusalem | | | | 10:27-39 |
| 113. Leaves Jerusalem And Goes To Perea | To Perea | | | | 10:40-42 |
| 114. Begins Perean Ministry That Leads Finally To Cross And Teaches | Perea | | | 13:22-30 | |
| 115. Faces Threat Of Pharisees And Of Herod And Declares Judgment On Jerusalem | Perea | | | 13:31-35 | |
| 116. Heals The Man With Dropsy (M #36) Amid Attacks By Pharisees And Teaches With The Parable OF The Wedding Feast And The Great Supper (P #19-20) | Perea | | | 14:1-24 | |
| 117. Begins First Perea Sermon (S #14) | Perea | | | 14:25-35 | |
| 118. Continues Sermon Using The Parables Of The Lost Sheep, The Lost Coin And The Lost Son And The Loving Father (P #21-23) | Perea | | | 15:1-32 | |
| 119. Continues Sermon (S #14) With Parable Of The Unjust Steward (P #24) And The Story Of Lazarus And The Rich Man | Perea | | | 16:1-31 | |
| 120. Finishes Sermon (S #14) With Some Words To His Disciples On Faith | Perea | | | 17:1-10 | |
| 121. Receives News Of Lazarus's Sickness And Tarries Two Days Though Lazarus Dies Before Leaving | Perea (Lazarus—Bethany) | | | | 11:1-16 |

| EVENT | PLACE | MT | MK | LK | JN |
|---|---|---|---|---|---|
| 122. Goes To Bethany And En-route Heals Ten Lepers (M #37) | Perea to road through Galilee (edge), Samaria, Jerusalem, Bethany | | | 17:11-19 | |
| 123. Raises Lazarus From The Dead (M #38) | Bethany | | | | 11:17-53 |
| 124. Returns By Same Route To Perea To Finish Ministry There And Make Last Journey To Jerusalem With Passover Crowds And There He Heals Many (M #39) | Bethany to Perea via Jerusalem, Samaria, Galilee (edge) to Northern Perea | 19:1-2 | 10:1 | | 11:54 |
| 125. Preaches The Second Perea Sermon (S #15) And Gives The Parables Of The Widow And The Unjust Judge and the Pharisee And The Publican (P # 25,26) | Perea | | | 17:20-18:14 | |
| 126. Teaches On Divorce | Perea | 19:3-12 | 10:2-12 | | |
| 127. Teaches On And Blesses Children | Perea | 19:13-15 | 10:13-16 | 18:15-17 | |
| 128. Has Discussion With The Rich Young Ruler (PE #5) | Perea | 19:16-22 | 10:17-22 | 18:18-27 | |
| 129. Gives Christian Rewards Discourse (PD #6) And Given the Parable Of The Laborers And The Vineyard (P #27) | Perea | 19:23-20:16 | 10:23-31 | 18:28-30 | |
| 130. Gives The Calvary Discourse (PD #7) | Perea (near Jordan) | 20:17-19 | 10:32-34 | 18:31-34 | |
| 131. Rebukes James And John For Ambition And Gives The Second Who-Is-Greatest Discourse (PD #8) (*Perea Rejects*) | Perea (near Jordan) | 20:20-28 | 10:35-45 | | |
| 132. Heals Blind Bartimaeus (M #40) | Jericho | 20:29-34 | 10:46-52 | 18:35-43 | |
| 133. Meets Zaccheus (PE #6) | After leaving Jericho on road to Jerusalem | | | 19:1-10 | |
| 134. Gives The Parable Of The Pounds (P #28) And Preaches The Jericho Sermon (S #16) | On road to Jerusalem | | | 19:11-27 | |
| 135. Arrives At Bethany And Is Anointed By Mary (*Friday, Nisan 8*) [*Passover 4 approaching*] | Bethany | 26:6-13 | 14:3-9 | | 11:55-12:11 |

## Last Days In Jerusalem (Spring 30 A.D.)

| | | | | | |
|---|---|---|---|---|---|
| **Saturday** | | | | | |
| 136. Enters Jerusalem In The Triumphal Entry | Bethany to Jerusalem | 21:1-11 | 11:1-11 | 19:28-44 | 12:12-19 |
| **Sunday** | | | | | |
| 137. Curses Barren Fig Tree | Road from Bethany to Jerusalem | 21:17-19 | 11:12-14 | | |
| 138. Cleanses Temple (M #41) And Heals Some | Jerusalem | **21:12-16** | 11:15-19 | 19:45-48 | |
| **Monday** | | | | | |
| 139. Sees Fig Tree Withered (M #42) (PD#9) | Road from Bethany to Jerusalem | 21:20-22 | 11:20-26 | | |
| 140. Faces Sanhedrin Questions And Preacher The Authority Sermon (S #17) (P #29-31) | Jerusalem | 21:23-22:14 | 11:27-12:12 | 20:1-19 | |
| 141. Faces Questions By Pharisees And Herodians About Taxes | Jerusalem | 22:15-22 | 12:13-17 | 20:20-26 | |
| 142. Faces Questions By Sadducees About The Resurrection | Jerusalem | 22:23-33 | 12:18-27 | 20:20-26 | |

| EVENT | PLACE | MT | MK | LK | JN |
|---|---|---|---|---|---|
| 143. Faces Questions By Pharisees About Greatest Commandment (PE #7) | Jerusalem | 22:34-40 | 12:28-34 | | |
| 144. Faces Questions By Pharisees About How Christ Is The Son Of David | Jerusalem | 22:41-46 | 12:35-37 | 20:41-44 | |
| 145. Preaches The Hypocrite Sermon (S #18) | Jerusalem | 23:1-39 | 12:38-40 | 20:45-47 | |
| 146. Speaks On The Widow's Mite | Jerusalem | | 12:41-44 | 21:1-4 | |
| 147. Faces Questions By Some Greeks And Speaks To The Father And The Father Answers | Jerusalem | | | | 12:20-36 |
| 148. Faces Rejection By Many With Some Believers Remaining Quiet | Jerusalem | | | | 12:37-43 |
| 149. Preaches The Last Evangelistic Sermon (S #19) | Jerusalem | | | | 12:44-50 |
| 150. Preaches The Olivet Discourse (PD #10) (P #32-34) (*Jerusalem Rejects*) | Mount of Olives near Jerusalem | 24:1-25:46 | 13:1-37 | 21:5-36 | |
| 151. Faces Sanhedrin Plotting His Death | Jerusalem | 26:1-5 | 14:1-2 | 22:1-2 | |
| **Tuesday** | | | | | |
| 152. Faces Judas Pursuing Betrayal | Jerusalem | 26:14-16 | 14:10-11 | 22:3-6 | |
| 153. Prepares For The Passover And Preliminary Meal | Jerusalem | 26:17-19 | 14:12-16 | 22:7-13 | |
| 154. Begins The Last Supper | Jerusalem (Upper Room) | | | | 13:1 |
| 155. Washes The Disciples Feet | Upper Room | | | | 13:2-17 |
| 156. Warns Of A Betrayer | Upper Room | 26:21-25 | 14:18-21 | 22:21-23 | 13:18-30 |
| 157. Institutes The Lord's Supper | Upper Room | 26:26-29 | 14:22-25 | **22:19-20** | |
| 158. Faces Disciples Argument Over Greatness | Upper Room | | | 22:24-30 | 13:31-35 |
| 159. Tells Of Peter's Coming Denial | Upper Room | | | 22:31-38 | 13:36-38 |
| 160. Gives His Comfort Discourse (PD #11) | Upper Room | | | | 14:1-31 |
| 161. Leaves Upper Room And Repeats Warning To Peter | Jerusalem | 26:30-35 | 14:26-31 | 22:39 | 14:31b |
| 162. Gives His Vine Branches Discourse (PD #12) | Jerusalem | | | | 15:1-16:33 |
| 163. Prays His High Priestly Prayer | Jerusalem | | | | 17:1-26 |
| 164. Enters Gethsemane Asking Peter, James and John To Pray | Garden of Gethsemane in Jerusalem | 26:36-37 | 14:32-33 | 22:40a | 18:1 |
| 165. Enters His Terrors And Finds Peter, James and John Sleeping Three Times | Garden of Gethsemane in Jerusalem | 26:38-46 | 14:34-42 | 22:40b-46 | |
| 166. Faces Mob And Judas' Betrayal And Proclaiming Himself The "I AM" (M #43) | Garden of Gethsemane in Jerusalem | 26:47-50 | 14:43-45 | 22:47-48 | 18:2-9 |
| 167. Heals Malchus' Ear After Peter Lobs It Off (M #44) | Garden of Gethsemane in Jerusalem | 26:51-54 | 14:46-47 | 22:49-51 | 18:10-11 |
| 168. Faces Arrest As Disciples Scatter And Is Led Away | Garden of Gethsemane in Jerusalem | 26:55-57 | 14:48-53 | 22:52-54 | 18:12-13a |

| EVENT | PLACE | MT | MK | LK | JN |
|---|---|---|---|---|---|
| 169. Faces Annas For First Trial As Peter Denys (PE #8) | Jerusalem | | | | 18:13-23 |
| 170. Faces Crowded Sanhedrin For Second Trial As Peter Continues Denial (PE #9) | Jerusalem at Caiaphas' house | 26:58-75 | 14:53-72 | 22:55-65 | 18:24-27 |
| **Wednesday**<br>171. Faces Third Trial And Is Convicted | Jerusalem | | | 22:66-71 | |
| 172. Faces Pilate For Fourth Trial (PE #10) | Jerusalem | 27:1-14 | 15:1-5 | 23:1-5 | 18:28-38 |
| 173. Faces Herod For Fifth Trial (PE #11) | Jerusalem | | | 23:6-12 | |
| 174. Faces Pilate Again For Sixth Trial (PE #12) | Jerusalem | 27:15-23 | 15:6-14 | 23:13-23 | 18:39-19:15 |
| 175. Receives Sentence Of Death (*Israel Reject*) | Jerusalem | 27:24-30 | 15:15-20 | 23:24-25 | 19:16 |
| 176. Is Taken To Calvary | Jerusalem | 27:31-34 | 15:21-22 | 23:26-32 | 19:17 |
| 177. Nailed To Cross And Suffers (Cry #1, 2, 3) (PE #13) | Calvary | 27:35-44 | 15:23-32 | 23:33-43 | 19:18-27 |
| 178. Suffers Darkness On Cross (Cry #4, 5, 6, 7) | Calvary | 27:45-49 | 15:33-36 | 23:44-46a | 19:28-30a |
| 179. Dies [DEATH] | Calvary | 27:50-53 | 15:37-38 | 23:46b | 19:30b |
| 180. Faces Piercing Of Side And Roman Soldier Speaks | Calvary | 27:54-56 | 15:39-41 | 23:47-49 | 19:31-37 |
| 181. Is Buried [BURIAL] | Calvary | 27:57-61 | 15:42-46 | 23:50-54 | 19:38-42 |
| **Thursday**<br>182. Has Tomb Sealed | Jerusalem | 27:62-66 | | 23:55-56 | |
| **Saturday**<br>183. Has Women Watch | Jerusalem | | 15:47 | | |
| **Sunday**<br>[RESURRECTION]<br>183. Resurrects And Mary Magdalene Finds Empty Tomb | Jerusalem | | | | 20:1-2 |
| 184. Has Peter And John Find His Tomb Empty | Jerusalem | | | | 20:3-10 |
| 185. Meets Mary Near Tomb (RA #1) (PE #14) | Jerusalem | | | | 20:11-18 |
| 186. Has Other Women Find His Tomb Empty | Jerusalem | 28:1-4 | 16:1-4 | 24:1-3 | |
| 187. Has Angel Tell Women Of Resurrection And Appear To Them (RA #2) | Jerusalem | 28:5-10 | 16:5-8 | 24:4-8 | |
| 188. Meets Peter (RA #3) | Jerusalem | | 16:9-11 | 24:9-12 | |
| 189. Meets Two On Emmaus Road (RA #4) (M #45) | Near Jerusalem | | 16:12-13 | 24:13-35 | |
| 190. Meets Ten Disciples (RA #5) (M #46) | Jerusalem | | | 24:36-43 | 20:19-25 |
| **Later Events**<br>191. Meets Eleven Disciples (RA #6) | Jerusalem | | | | 20:26-31 |
| 192. Re-commissions The Fisherman Disciples (RA #7) (M #47) | Jerusalem | | | | 21:1-25 |
| 193. Meets The 500 And Gives The Great Commission (RA #8) | Galilee | 28:16-20 | | | |
| 194. Meets The Eleven Disciples Again And Repeats Great Commission (RA #9) | Jerusalem | | 16:14-18 | 24:44-49 | |
| 195. Ascends To Heaven (RA #10) (M #48) | Mountain Near Jerusalem | | 16:19-20 | 24:50-53 | |

# A Guide the Harmony of the Gospels

- *Italicized* numbers mean there is a corresponding note in this section.
- **Bolded** references mean this event is out of chronological order in this Gospel.
- (Parenthesis) refers to other charts in this volume.
- **M** = Miracle, **PE** = Personal Encounter, **S** = Sermon,
  **P** = Parable, **PD** = Private Discourse,
  **RA** = Resurrection Appearance,
  **Cry** = Cry of Christ On the Cross

⬅──────────────➡

## Notes:

**41.** Luke 5:1-11 is often listed as paralleling Matthew 4:18-22 and Mark 1:16-20, but this is a separate event after Jesus called the four fishermen. In Luke 5, the four fishermen leave the fishing business completely to follow Christ whereas the earlier event was just a general call that did not mean they were fully out of their profession. In Matthew and Mark, we have two separate episodes for two sets of brothers while in Luke all are together and there is a miracle.

**51.** John 5:1-47 is given in John during a time of Christ's ministry that John's Gospel omits (besides here and the healing of the Nobleman's Son in 4:46-54). The inclusion of this story in John is no doubt to help us relate that another year has passed as it is now the second Passover of His ministry.

**63.** Luke 11:14-16 is often listed here as paralleling Matthew 12:22-45 and Mark 3:20-30, but this is a separate event where a similar episode to the one here in Capernaum happens, probably, in Perea.

**64.** Luke does have the episode involving Jesus' mother and brethren in a different order (Luke. 8:19-20). It was a simultaneous event with the preaching of the Kingdom of Heaven Parables Sermon. In other words, it was an interruption.

**65.** Matthew 8:19-22 is often listed as paralleling Luke 9:57-62, but these are similar incidents at a different place and time that probably happened often in Christ's ministry.

**75.** We have the Feeding of the 5000 listed as taking place in Bethsaida Julius. We know this because Mark 6:24 says that they were in the midst of the Sea while John 6:19 says that they were 25-30 furlongs (3.5 to 3.75 miles) across the Sea. Also, John 6:1 pinpoints it as "the other side of the Sea of Galilee", so this is not the Bethsaida of Galilee where Peter once lived.

**76.** After the return toward Bethsaida in Galilee, Jesus and the Twelve land in Gennesarrat where many are healed (Miracle #23). They either landed in Bethsaida and walked to Gennesarrat, or, more likely, Jesus had just indicated the general direction (west) and then specified after they miraculously landed on shore. We believe there are clearly two places named Bethsaida in the Gospels—Bethsaida of Galilee on the western shore and Bethsaida Julius on the eastern shore technically in Decapolis.

**78.** Notice the change in Christ's ministry during "The Late Great Ministry in Galilee" after Jesus preaches the Bread of Life Sermon (Sermon #7). This basically stops the Galilean ministry and Galilee thoroughly rejects. From here to the exit of Galilee and the commencement of "The Ministry in Perea and Toward Jerusalem", there is keen opposition and Jesus spends most of the time outside of Galilee (north in Phoenicia, northeast in Caesarea Philippi, and east in Decapolis which are all out of the territories of Herod Antipas). The frenzied crowds after the Feeding of the 5000 (Miracle #21) made for a political problem. During this time, Jesus puts great emphasis on special teaching and training for the Twelve. Some call this time "The Retirement Ministry".

**89.** The Retirement Ministry ends with the Transfiguration. The amount of time from here to the end of the "Late Great Ministry in Galilee" was likely but a few days.

**97.** Matthew 8:19-22 and Luke 9:57-62 are the second and third time respectively that Christ has given these similar challenges in very similar incidents. Even we who serve Christ today surely notice how such "similar" situations often present themselves. As Christ, let us consider giving the same counsel.

**107.** Luke 11:14-36 is often listed parallel to a similar event at least a year earlier in Matthew 12:22-45. As likely happened often, the charge of working through Beelzebub was leveled against Him and He consistently answered as here.

**120.** As stated on the chart "The Public Sermons of Jesus", this sermon ("The First Perea Sermon") was perhaps more than one sermon, perhaps actually a series of sermons. There is the possibility, too, that He repeated this preaching at various places in Perea. We simply do not know, and in that the Gospel of Luke presents it without any breaks, we consider it a connected unit.

**121.** John 11:1-16 records the story of Lazarus. It seems hard to believe this journey is made in one day (one day for the servant to arrive, two days of tarrying, and then Jesus and the Twelve in one day of travel get to Bethany). To get to what was a border of Galilee seems difficult. But likely the people's designation of the area did not match Rome's. Scythopolis is one of the 10 cities of Decapolis and is the only one west of the Jordan that adds land to the administrative district of Decapolis. The Jews though likely saw the area in the city of Scythopolis as part of Decapolis, but all the surrounding area as southern Galilee in their common conversation. The Bible speaks of leaving Galilee and entering Perea which can't be done without going through Decapolis unless the Jews didn't see the area as such. Jesus came from near the border of Perea and Galilee (technically Decapolis) and used a shorter way through Samaria healing the Ten Lepers at one rest stop. This fits the facts and beautifully harmonizes the Gospel record.

**124.** Matthew 19:1 is not when Christ left Galilee at the end of Late Great Ministry in Galilee, but after the end of time in Judea which Matthew doesn't discuss. Jesus goes to the top of Perea and over into the southern part of Galilee to begin the long, slow descent through Perea toward Jerusalem. Mark 10:1 refers to the way He travels to Jerusalem on His last journey, not how He got to northern Perea as in Matthew 19:1.

**135.** The story of Mary anointing Jesus does raise some difficulties in making a harmony. John's Gospel must be correct in chronology as the day is given so specifically (John 12:1, "Six days before the Passover") and then for the Triumphal Entry (John 12:12. "on the next day"). Both Matthew and Mark, which are chronological at this point, do in this instance tell the story out of place. The purpose, apparently, to compare Mary to the religious rulers as well as to give a background for Judas whose true colors were clear at least four days before he took the awful steps to go to Jesus' enemies to see what he could receive for betraying Christ. Note also how Matthew and Mark both use language of imprecise times and speak actually of reading back to tell a story at an appropriate place in the narrative. Matthew 26:6 says, "Now when Jesus was in Bethany, in the house of Simon the leper", and so was referring to days before. Mark 14:3 uses similar words.

**137.** In regards to Jesus cursing the Barren Fig Tree, it appears that Matthew and Mark reverse the order. Mark, it appears, gives the true order—cursing the fig tree on the way to cleanse the temple. Matthew, usually chronological at this point, takes on the event of the previous day in 21: 18-19 so that he might tell the story of that day in verses 20-22. "Now" in 21:18 is a favorite word of Matthew (Strong's #1161, and can mean "also or moreover"). The word "presently" in 21:19 means "immediately" and so Matthew's emphasis is that the miracle was, as usual, instantaneous, though it was the next day that the Disciples had the privilege of seeing it. The word "soon" in verse 20 is the same word and the word can mean either. In essence, it was "immediately", and even to the Disciples it was "soon".

**139.** Matthew tells us the story of the cursed fig tree as one story so that the whole episode may be considered at once. Mark gives the precise order as the tree was cursed on Sunday, and then noticed in its withered state on Monday.

**153.** Matthew 26:17, Mark 14:12 and Luke 22:7 speak of the Day of Unleavened Bread as being at hand as well as the Passover. Remember, to the Jew the next day began at sunset and so Wednesday began soon and is the day to kill the lambs. This Last Supper is a preliminary meal the night before. Passover lambs were actually slain as Jesus was dying. The reason He has to be off the cross at sunset is for the Passover meal to be held. Remember also, that all of our charts in this volume are converted to midnight bringing in a new day as we are accustomed to in our culture.

**157.** Luke doesn't follow Matthew and Mark here and tells of the Institution of the Lord's Supper after the warning of the betrayer. We believe Matthew and Mark to be chronological as the betrayer needed to be gone before the Lord's Supper. Luke is really just in a discussion of the Supper including its institution, and then brings us up to date on the betrayer.

You can also use the statistics from this Harmony to see the interaction between the Gospels and emphases within them.

### Figure 10: Statistics of the Gospels

## Statistics of the Gospels

### Book Comparisons

| Book | # of Chapters | % of Chapters | # of Verses | % of Verses | # of Words | % of Words |
|---|---|---|---|---|---|---|
| Matthew | 28 | 31% | 1,071 | 28% | 23,343 | 28% |
| Mark | 16 | 18% | 678 | 18% | 14,949 | 18% |
| Luke | 24 | 27% | 1,151 | 31% | 25,640 | 31% |
| John | 21 | 24% | 879 | 23% | 18,658 | 23% |
| Total | 89 | 100% | 3,779 | 100% | 82,590 | 100% |

Using the **KJV**

### Harmony Items Involving Each Gospel

| Book | # Represented Out of 195 | % Involved In Total Harmony |
|---|---|---|
| Matthew | 99 | 51% |
| Mark | 91 | 47% |
| Luke | 123 | 63% |
| John | 64 | 33% |

### Breakdown of Harmony Items

| | |
|---|---|
| Matthew Alone 13 | Mark/Luke 7 |
| Mark Alone 3 | Mark/John 0 |
| Luke Alone 43 | Luke/John 3 |
| John Alone 39 | Matthew/Mark/Luke 43 |
| Matthew/Mark 15 | Matthew/Luke/John 0 |
| Matthew/Luke 7 | Mark/Luke/John 0 |
| Matthew/John 0 | Matthew/Mark/John 3 |
| | Total 195 |

**Notes:**
1. Any Harmony is somewhat arbitrary in how it breaks down the passages, and some books counting a passage may be much briefer than another. We use here our harmony that has 195 unique items.
2. Still, this gives us some idea of uniqueness.
3. Luke is largest and has the most unique items on the harmony. Matthew/Mark/Luke is the largest combination with 43 out of 195 items. These 3 together are the Synoptic Gospels.

## Special Pedagogical Methods of Jesus

The student of the Gospels will notice some special elements of teaching that Jesus employed that really defined His earthly ministry. They all involved relating to people in some way.

Jesus made use of parables in a way that is duplicated nowhere else in Scripture. These parables were a special, effective teaching device that powerfully presented the great truths the Lord shared. In addition, on a level unparalleled in other parts of the Bible, there are also, many miracles performed by Christ. They play deeply into the mission Christ came to carry out.

Jesus ministered to people. That ministry was in three spheres. He preached in public the greatest sermons ever preached. In addition, He taught the small band of His Disciples with some amazing personal discourses to them. Finally, there are several extraordinary personal encounters with individuals. There were many more in all these categories than what the Gospels record, but what is presented is exactly what the Holy Spirit has given us for its life-changing effects.

Because of the glorious significance of the death, burial, and resurrection of Christ, we see that the Gospels pause to give us seven cries of Christ from His cross. Further instruction is found when we trace the resurrection appearances of Christ that also show that many witnessed our Resurrected Savior.

Please review the following:

## Figures 11-17

- **The Recorded Parables of Jesus Christ**
- **The Recorded Miracles of Jesus Christ**
- **The Public Sermons of Jesus**
- **The Private Discourses of Jesus with the Disciples**
- **The Personal Encounters of Jesus**
- **The Cries of Christ on the Cross**
- **The Post-Resurrection Appearances of Christ**

## Figure 11

### The Recorded Parables of Jesus Christ*

| | Parable | Matthew | Mark | Luke | John |
|---|---|---|---|---|---|
| 1. | The Garments and Bottles | 9:16-17 | 2:21-22 | 5:36-39 | |
| 2. | The Two Houses | 7:24-27 | | 6:47-49 | |
| 3. | The Two Debtors | | | 7:41-42 | |
| 4. | The Sower | 13:1-23 | 4:1-20 | 8:4-15 | |
| 5. | The Wheat and the Tares | 13:24-30 | | | |
| 6. | The Mustard Seed | 13:31-32 | 4:30-32 | 13:18-19 | |
| 7. | The Leaven | 13:33 | | 13:20-21 | |
| 8. | The Hidden Treasure | 13:44 | | | |
| 9. | The Pearl of Great Price | 13:45-46 | | | |
| 10. | The Fishing Net | 13:47-50 | | | |
| 11. | The Scribe and the Householder | 13:50-51 | | | |
| 12. | The Growing Seed | | 4:26-29 | | |
| 13. | The Unforgiving Servant | 18:23-35 | | | |
| 14. | The Good Samaritan | | | 10:25-37 | |
| 15. | The Persistent Friend | | | 11:1-10 | |
| 16. | The Rich Fool | | | 12:16-21 | |
| 17. | The Faithful Stewards | | | 12:42-48 | |
| 18. | The Barren Fig Tree | | | 13:6-9 | |
| 19. | The Wedding Feast | | | 14:7-14 | |
| 20. | The Great Supper | | | 14:15-24 | |
| 21. | The Lost Sheep | | | 15:3-7 | |
| 22. | The Lost Coin | | | 15:8-10 | |
| 23. | The Lost Son and the Loving Father | | | 15:11-32 | |
| 24. | The Unjust Steward | | | 16:1-13 | |
| 25. | The Widow and the Unjust Judge | | | 18:1-8 | |
| 26. | The Pharisee and the Publican | | | 18:9-14 | |
| 27. | The Laborers in the Vineyard | 20:1-16 | | | |
| 28. | The Pounds | | | 19:11-27 | |
| 29. | The Two Sons | 21:28-32 | | | |
| 30. | The Dishonest Husbandmen | 21:33-40 | 12:1-9 | 20:9-19 | |
| 31. | The Marriage of the King's Son | 22:1-14 | | | |
| 32. | The Fig Tree and the Future | 24:32-35 | 13:28-31 | 21:29-33 | |
| 33. | The Ten Virgins | 25:1-13 | | | |
| 34. | The Talents | 25:14-30 | | | |

\* *This includes only parables and not metaphors, similitudes or allegories. Some of the above are smaller parables but the Scripture itself calls them parables.*

## Figure 12

### The Recorded Miracles of Jesus Christ

| Miracle | Matthew | Mark | Luke | John |
|---|---|---|---|---|
| 1. Turning Water Into Wine | | | | 2:1-11 |
| 2. Healing the Nobleman's Son | | | | 4:46-54 |
| 3. Vanishing From a Hostile Multitude | | | 4:16-32 | |
| 4. Healing a Demon Possessed Man at a Synagogue | | 1:23-24 | 4:33-36 | |
| 5. Healing Peter's Mother-in-law | 8:14-15 | 1:29-31 | 4:38-40 | |
| 6. Healing Many Sick One Evening | 8:16-17 | 1:32-34 | 4:40-41 | |
| 7. Catching First Draught of Fishes | | | 5:1-11 | |
| 8. Cleansing a Leper | 8:1-4 | 1:40-45 | 5:12-15 | |
| 9. Healing the Man With Palsy | 9:2-7 | 2:3-12 | 5:18-25 | |
| 10. Healing the Impotent Man | | | | 5:1-9 |
| 11. Healing the Man With the Withered Hand | 12:9-14 | 3:1-6 | 6:6-10 | |
| 12. Healing Many In A Multitude | 12:15-21 | 3:7-12 | | |
| 13. Healing the Centurions Servant | 8:5-13 | | 7:1-10 | |
| 14. Raising a Widow's Son from the Dead | | | 7:11-18 | |
| 15. Calming the Storm | 8:23-27 | 4:35-41 | 8:22-25 | |
| 16. Healing the Maniac of Gadara & Demons In Swine | 8:28-31 | 5:1-20 | 8:26-27 | |
| 17. Healing the Woman with an Issue of Blood | 9:18-22 | 5:25-34 | 8:43-48 | |
| 18. Raising Jairus' Daughter from the Dead | 9:23-26 | 5:22-43 | 8:41-56 | |
| 19. Healing the Two Blind Men | 9:27-31 | | | |
| 20. Healing the Demon Possessed Mute Man | 9:32-34 | | | |
| 21. Feeding the Five Thousand and Healing | 14:13-20 | 6:31-44 | 9:10-17 | 6:1-14 |
| 22. Walking on the Sea & Stopping the Storm | 14:22-33 | 6:45-52 | | 6:5-21 |
| 23. Healing Many at Gennesaret After the Storm | 14:34-36 | 6:53-56 | | |
| 24. Healing of the Syro-Phoenician Woman's Daughter | 15:21-28 | 7:24-30 | | |
| 25. Healing the Deaf and Speech-Impaired Man | | 7:31-37 | | |
| 26. Healing Others at Decapolis | 15:29-31 | | | |
| 27. Feeding the Four Thousand | 15:32-38 | 8:1-9 | | |
| 28. Healing the Blind Man at Bethsaida Julius | | 8:22-26 | | |
| 29. Transfiguring upon a Mountain | 17:1-13 | 9:1-13 | 9:28-36 | |
| 30. Healing the Possessed Boy Who Had Seizures | 17:14-20 | 9:14-29 | 9:37-43 | |
| 31. Getting a Coin from a Fishes Mouth for Taxes | 17:24-27 | | | |
| 32. Vanishing Again From A Murderous Mob | | | | 8:59 |
| 33. Healing the Man Born Blind | | | | 9:1-41 |
| 34. Casting Out A Demon | | | 11:14-15 | |
| 35. Healing the Infirm, Bent-Over Woman | | | 13:10-17 | |
| 36. Healing the Man With Dropsy | | | 14:1-6 | |
| 37. Healing the Ten Lepers | | | 17:11-19 | |
| 38. Raising Lazarus from the Dead | | | | 11:1-46 |

| Miracle | Matthew | Mark | Luke | John |
|---|---|---|---|---|
| 39. Healing Many In Perea | 19:1-2 | | | |
| 40. Healing Blind Bartimaus | 20:29-34 | 10:46-52 | 18:35-43 | |
| 41. Healing Blind & Lame At Temple After Cleansing | 21:12-16 | | | |
| 42. Withering the Fig Tree | 21:17-22 | 11:12-24 | | |
| 43. Knocking Down the Mob at His Arrest | | | | 18:1-6 |
| 44. Healing Malchus' Ear | | | | 18:7-14 |
| 45. Vanishing From Two on Emmaus Road | | | 24:31 | |
| 46. Entering a Room Through a Closed Door | | | | 20:19-23 |
| 47. Catching Second Draught of Fishes | | | | 21:1-14 |
| 48. Ascending To Heaven | | 16:19-20 | 24:50-52 | |

**Notes:**

*1. The criteria for being listed here is that the miracle was performed by Jesus Christ and had to be witnessed by someone. For example, the actual miracles of the Resurrection and the Virgin Birth were not witnessed by anyone and therefore are not included in this list.*

*2. Some miracles listed actually contain multiple miracles in one story. For example, in Miracle #22, Jesus saw through a storm to the sea from a mountain, He walked on the sea, He allowed Peter to walk on the sea, He rescued Peter, He stopped the storm, and He miraculously got from the middle of the sea to the shore in a moment.*

*3. #17 and #18 are part of the same story, but #17 was actually the first miracle of the two.*

# Notes

# Figure 13

## The Public Sermons of Jesus

| The Sermon | Location & Audience | Subject | Result | Reference |
|---|---|---|---|---|
| 1. The First Sermon | At the synagogue in Nazareth to the hometown crowd. | Explains Himself as the fulfillment of Isaiah 61 and addresses their rejection and jealousy. | Took Him out of the city to push Him off a cliff, but He vanished to escape. | Luke 4:16-30 |
| 2. The First Evangelistic Sermon | At Jerusalem at His first Passover after healing the man at Pool of Bethesda to Jews present. | Explains that salvation is in Him. | No reaction given but He leaves for Galilee. | John 5:17-47 |
| 3. The Sermon On The Mount | On a mountain near Capernaum to His followers. | Teaches how to live as a subject of His kingdom. | The people were astonished, but followed Him down. | Matt. 5-7 Luke 6:20-49 |
| 4. The Personal Responsibility Sermon | In Galilee to a multitude as John the Baptist's two disciples arrived. | Explains not to draw the wrong conclusion, but see the greater issue of their own hearts and ending with a great invitation. | Pharisees and scribes reject, but ask Him to eat. | Matt. 11:7-30 Luke 7:29-35 |
| 5. The Rejection Sermon | In Capernaum to the crowd with much interruption by the Pharisees. | Explains what is rejection and what is really of Satan. | The Pharisees blasphemed the Holy Ghost and thereby committed the unpardonable sin. | Matt. 12:22-45 |
| 6. The Kingdom of Heaven Parables Sermon | Sitting in a boat on Galilee to a multitude. | Teaches the mysteries of His kingdom for those who have the heart for it. | They tried to understand "as they were able to hear it". | Matt. 13:1-53 Mark 4:1-34 Luke 8:1-18 |
| 7. The Bread of Life Sermon | In Capernaum to multitude. | Preaches boldly that He is the only Bread, the only way to Heaven. | Many followers left and no more walked with Him. | John 6:26-66 |
| 8. The Defilement Sermon | Near Capernaum to a crowd nearby to the Pharisees with whom He was speaking. | Teaches what really defiles a man. | No response by the crowd, but disciples ask for more explanation in private. | Matt. 15:10-11 Mark 7:14-16 |
| 9. The Living Water Sermon | In Galilee to His followers with some Pharisees present. | Explains that He is the Living Water and then offered to all. | Pharisees argued and some others believed. The people were divided. | John 7:14-53 |

| The Sermon | Location & Audience | Subject | Result | Reference |
|---|---|---|---|---|
| 10. The "I AM" Sermon | A confrontation with the Pharisees turned into a sermon at the temple. | Teaches that He is the Great "I Am" while they are of the Devil. Also explains that He is the Light of the World. | Sermon interrupted by the woman taken in adultery episode. They took up stones to stone Him and He miraculously escapes. | John 8:1-59 |
| 11. The Good Shepherd Sermon | To a crowd in Jerusalem. | Teaches that He is the Good Shepherd and the only Door to the sheep. | The crowd was divided in their opinion. | John 9:39-10:21 |
| 12. The Christian Workers Sermon | To the 70 as they were leaving to serve near Jerusalem. | Teaches the way of Christian service and what to expect. | The 70 left to serve and returned later rejoicing. Jesus closed with a prayer and a word to the Twelve. | Luke 10:1-24 |
| 13. The Sermon On The Plain | To His followers somewhere in Judea. | Repeats part of the Sermon on the Mount and shows what is really important in life and what is truly spiritual. | No response given except for Peter asking a question. | Luke 12:1-59 |
| 14. The First Perean Sermon (perhaps multiple sermons in #14 & #15, but given in Luke with no breaks) | To His followers and the Pharisees and scribes who followed on the journey through Perea. | Teaches much on the heart of God in the first parable and on the terror of hell in the story of Lazarus and the rich man. | Pharisees constantly interrupt and at the end, the 12 ask Him to "Increase our faith". | Luke 14:25-17:10 |
| 15. The Second Perean Sermon | To His followers after the Pharisees demanded an answer on journey through Perea. | Teaches on various subjects as there is little time left for preaching. | They brought infants for Him to touch. | Luke 17:22-18:14 |
| 16. The Jericho Sermon | To His followers in Jericho on last trip to Jerusalem. | Teaches on the service they need to give Him in the future. | None given but they continue on. | Luke 19:11-27 |
| 17. The Authority Sermon | To the crowd with Pharisees and Scribes trying to trap Him. | Teaches on real authority and through parables on how they will answer to Him. | None given, but Pharisees went to counsel further on how they might entangle Him. | Matt. 21:23-22:14 Mark 11:27-12:12 Luke 20:1-19 |
| 18. The Hypocrite Sermon | To His followers in Jerusalem. | Teaches the danger of hypocrisy as demonstrated by the Pharisees. | None given. | Matt. 23:1-39 Mark 12:38-40 Luke 20:45-47 |
| 19. The Last Evangelistic Sermon | In Jerusalem to those near the Temple. | On His last opportunity, He cries out that they believe on Him as He reminds them He has spoken as the Father desires. | None given. | John 12:44-50 |

# Figure 14

## The Personal Discourses Of Jesus With The Disciples

| The Discourse | Location & Setting | Subject | Result | Reference |
|---|---|---|---|---|
| 1. The Fields White For Harvest Discourse | In Samaria after dealing with the woman at the well. (The Twelve not yet called) | Explains that His work drives Him as there are so many who need Him. | None recorded but went on to see great results after the woman at the well witnessed. | Jn. 4:31-38 |
| 2. The Sending Out Discourse | In Galilee when He was sending out the Twelve for service. (From here forward the Twelve were officially called) | Explains all that is really involved in being a servant of Him. | They went out to serve. The results were the valuable training they received. | Mk. 6:7-13 Mt. 10:1-42 |
| 3. The Soul Versus The Whole World Discourse | In Caesara Philippi to the 12 though a few others listened. | Explains the value of the soul compared to all this life has to offer. | From here He took Peter, James, and John to the Mount of Transfiguration | Mt. 16:24-28 Mk. 8:34- 9:1 Lk. 9:23-26 |
| 4. The First Who-Is-The-Greatest Discourse | In Capernaum after a miracle. | Explains how Jesus sees who is the greatest among men. | They went on, but later chapters in Matthew show they did not take this discourse to heart. | Mt. 18:1-35 Mk. 9:33-50 Lk. 9:46-56 |
| 5. The Prayer Discourse | In Judea. | Explains how to pray and gives the model prayer. | None given, but in book of Acts they put to use. | Lk. 11:1-13 |
| 6. The Christian Rewards Discourse | In Perea. | Explains how He will disperse rewards. | Later verses prove this is an area where little progress is made. | Mt. 19:23-20:16 Mk. 10:23-31 Lk. 18:28-30 |
| 7. The Calvary Discourse | Near Jordan. | Explains that they go to Jerusalem for His death, burial and resurrection. | Their minds are still on rewards and honor for themselves as later verses show they did not understand | Mt. 20:17-19 Mk. 10:32-34 Lk. 18:31-34 |
| 8. The Second Who-Is-The-Greatest Discourse | Still near Jordan. | Explains that to be the greatest you must be a servant. | They went on to Jerusalem with no response to the discourse. | Mt. 20:20-28 Mk. 10:35-45 |
| 9. The Fig Tree Discourse | On road from Bethany to Jerusalem. | Explains that fruit is needed and not leaves only, and that faith is essential for this fruit. | None given as the events of those days were a whirlwind. | Mt. 21:18-22 Mk. 11:20-26 |
| 10. The Olivet Discourse | On the Mount of Olives To His Disciples | Teaches on the future with a great overview of prophecy. | None given. | Mt. 24:1-25:46 Mk. 13:1-37 Lk. 21:5-36 |
| 11. The Comfort Discourse | In the Upper Room. | Explains about Heaven and that He will not leave them comfortless. | None given but they leave the Upper Room. | Jn. 14:1-31 |
| 12. The Vine And The Branches Discourse | On the way to Gethsemene. | Explains that He is the Vine and we are the branches and that we must abide in Him. More given on the Comforter. | Apparently none, and Jesus goes into His High Priestly prayer for His own. | Jn. 15:1-16:33 |

# Notes

**Figure 15**

## The Personal Encounters of Jesus

| THE PERSON | LOCATION | SUBJECT OF DISCUSSION | RESULT | REFERENCE |
|---|---|---|---|---|
| 1. Nicodemus | Jerusalem | Nicodemus comes at night to talk with Jesus but the Lord turns the situation to the new birth Nicodemus needs. | Christ gives some of His greatest teaching on salvation. His later support of Jesus (John 7:50, 19:39) shows that he apparently accepted Christ. | John 3:1-21 |
| 2. The Woman At the Well | Sychar in Samaria | Jesus initiates a conversation with her and shows her the need of her heart | She accepts Him and testifies of the fact to the men of the city. | John 4:1-42 |
| 3. Three Insincere Disciples | Near Jordan | Three men offer to be Disciples and Jesus comments to them. | Jesus' comments suggest they were not sincere and did not follow. | Luke 9:57-62 |
| 4. The Woman Taken In Adultery | Jerusalem | As He teaches, the scribes and Pharisees bring the woman caught in adultery wanting to stone her. The man is not brought as they are using her to get to Jesus. After He says, "He that is without sin among you, let him first cast a stone at her," all leave. Then He initiates a conversation with her. | She receives His forgiveness. | John 8:1-11 |
| 5. The Rich Young Ruler | Perea | The young man came asking what things he could do to "inherit" eternal life. Jesus explained that he couldn't pay as he too was a sinner before the Lord. | He left sad because he valued his possessions over Christ. | Matt. 19:16-22 Mark 10:17-22 Luke 18:18-27 |
| 6. Zacchaeus | Near Jericho | He climbed a sycamore tree to see Jesus and Jesus initiated a conversation with him. Jesus went to his home. | Salvation came to him that day. | Luke 19:1-10 |
| 7. A Scribe | Jerusalem | In what began as an effort by the scribes and Pharisees to trap Jesus became a good discussion about the greatest commandment. The Scribe chosen talked one on one with Jesus. | Apparently, he saw the truth of Jesus' statements and Jesus told him he was not far from the Kingdom of God. | Matt. 22:34-40 Mark 12:28-34 |

| The Person | Location | Subject of Discussion | Result | Reference |
|---|---|---|---|---|
| 8. Annas | Jerusalem | During the first phase of Jesus' trial, He was taken to Annas while a quorum was being gathered for the Sanhedrin. He questioned Jesus. | Jesus boldly answered him as he was no longer the High Priest. An officer struck Jesus. | John 18:13-14, 19-23 |
| 9. Caiaphas | Jerusalem | Before the Sanhedrin during the trial Caiaphas rose to question Jesus. Jesus would not answer except in the one case where He could not deny Himself. | Caiaphas tore his clothes and accused Jesus of blasphemy. He is declared guilty. | Matt. 26:62-64 Mark 14:60-65 |
| 10. Pilate | Jerusalem | In the first of His civil trials, Pilate questions Jesus and Jesus will not speak for Himself. | Pilate declares "I find no fault in him." | Matt. 27:11-14 Mark 15:1-5 Luke 23:3 John 18:33-38 |
| 11. Herod | Jerusalem | Sent by Pilate, Herod questions Jesus and Jesus said nothing. | Herod made a mocking of the whole affair. | Luke 23:6-12 |
| 12. Pilate (again) | Jerusalem | Jesus is sent back to Pilate who questions him again. Jesus does not defend Himself. | Pilate attempts to get Jesus released but lacks the courage to do what he knew was right. Jesus is condemned. | Matt. 27:15-23 Mark 15:6-14 Luke 23:13-23 Jn 18:39-19:15 |
| 13. The Thief | On a cross beside Him on Calvary in Jerusalem | The thief, who first railed on Jesus as the crowd and another thief did, asks to be remembered in Jesus' Kingdom. | Jesus tells him, "To day shalt thou be with me in paradise." | Luke 23:39-45 |
| 14. Mary Magdalene | Jerusalem | A weeping Mary met Jesus near the empty tomb as she confused Him as the gardener. When He says her name she realizes to Whom she is speaking. | She goes and tells of the Resurrection to the Twelve. | John 20:11-18 |

**Notes:**

1. This list does not include the many discussions He had with the Twelve. Not even the one-on-one discussions with them are mentioned here. They received more of His discussions than anyone.
2. This list also does not include any encounter or discussion where a miracle or parable was involved though Jesus said many wonderful things at those times. This chart seeks to fill in the gap for those not on the parable or miracle listings. Particularly in the miracles He said many things personal to someone. Think, for example, of His discussions with both Martha and Mary during the episode of the raising of Lazarus.

**Figure 16**

## THE CRIES OF CHRIST ON THE CROSS

**1) The Forgiving Cry**
*"Father, forgive them; for they know not what they do" (Luke 23:34)*

**2) The Salvation Cry**
*"Verily I say unto thee, to day shalt thou be with me in paradise" (Luke 23:43)*

**3) The Caring Cry**
*"Woman, behold thy son! Behold thy mother" (John 19:26,27)*

**4) The Orphan Cry**
*"My God, my God, why have thou forsaken me?" (Matthew 27:46)*

**5) The Suffering Cry**
*"I thirst" (John 19:28)*

**6) The Victory Cry**
*"It is finished" (John 19:30)*

**7) The Final Cry**
*"Father, into thy hands I commend my spirit" (Luke 23:46)*

## THE PATHETIC SCENES OF JESUS' LAST DAYS

**1. The Scene of Failure and Strain**
~ *Among His own disciples (Mt. 26:20-56; Mk. 14:17-50; Lk. 22:14-53; Jn. 13:1-18:12)*

**2. The Scene of Abuse and Mockery**
~ *Before the Jewish Sanhedrin (Mt. 26:57-75; Mk. 14:51-72; Lk. 22:54-22:71; Jn. 18:13-27)*

**3. The Scene of Cowardice and Injustice**
~ *Before Pilate (Mt. 27:1-26; Mk. 15:1-21; Lk. 23:1-23:26; Jn. 18:28-19:16)*

**4. The Scene of Violence and Love**
~ *Before the Gaping Crowd (Mt. 27:27-66; Mk. 15:22-47; Lk. 23:27-56; Jn. 19:17-42)*

## THE VOICE FROM HEAVEN TO CHRIST

**1. The Voice For Authenticity At The Baptism Of Christ**
*"And lo a voice from heaven, saying, This is my beloved Son, in whom I am well pleased." (Mt 3:17)*

**2. The Voice For Preeminence At The Transfiguration Of Christ**
*"While he yet spake, behold, a bright cloud overshadowed them: and behold a voice out of the cloud, which said, This is my beloved Son, in whom I am well pleased; hear ye him." (Mt. 17:5)*

**3. The Voice For Encouragement As Christ Prepared To Become Sin For Us**
*"Father, glorify thy name. Then came there a voice from heaven, saying, I have both glorified it, and will glorify it again." (Jn. 12:28)*

# Figure 17

## The Post-Resurrection Appearances Of Jesus

| Appearance | Text | Features |
|---|---|---|
| 1. Mary Magdalene | John 20:11-17 | He appears first to a woman which shows the accuracy of God's Word as women were not even counted as witnesses then. She did not know Him at first. She sees the empty tomb. |
| 2. A Group of Women | Matthew 28:9-10 | They see the empty tomb and see angel. They touch Him. |
| 3. Peter | Mark 16:9-11; Luke 24:9-12, 34; I Corinthians 15:5 | He sees the empty tomb and grave clothes. |
| 4. Two On the Emmaus Road | Mark 16:12-13; Luke 24:13-35 | They ate with Him. They did not know Him at first. |
| 5. Ten of the Eleven Disciples | Luke 24:36-43; John 20:19-23 | He ate with them. He offered to let them touch Him and they see the wounds in His hands and feet. |
| 6. To All Eleven Disciples | John 20:26-31 | As before, He ate with them and allowed them to touch Him and His wounds. Thomas, left out before, cried out "My Lord and My God." |
| 7. To Peter, John and Five Other Disciples | John 21:1-25 | He made the meal and ate with them. |
| 8. The Disciples and Five Hundred Brethren | Matthew 28:16-20; I Corinthians 15:6 | This is the one planned appearance (Mt. 28:7). Here He gave the Great Commission. |
| 9. James and Other Ten | Mark 16:14-18; Luke 24:44-49 | Apparently spoke to James alone first. He ate with them. |
| 10. Those Assembled At His Ascension | Mark 16:19-20; Luke 24:50-53; Acts 1:4-11 | He promised to return in like manner. |
| 11. Paul | I Corinthians 15:8 | Paul was one "born out of due time". |

Notes:
1. Notice that Jesus only appeared to believers and never to unbelievers after His resurrection. It is faith and not sight as the Kingdom of God "cometh not by observation". Also notice that this does not include when Christ allowed others to see Him while He was not upon the earth—so neither Stephen at his stoning, nor John receiving the vision that is the Book of Revelation, are included.
2. He was seen and heard in every appearance. He was touched in at least 3 appearances. He even ate in 4 appearances.

## Synthesis of Key Events

The final study involving chronology of the Gospels is to look more deeply at those events that have especially moved the hearts of Christians over the years. The Gospels themselves will place a distinct emphasis on these same events. These events include the birth and infancy of Christ, the Upper Room and Gethsemane, the Trial of Christ, the Crucifixion, and the Resurrection. Here are the charts to do extra study on these key events of the Gospels:

## Figures 18-22

- **Synthesis of the Birth and Infancy of Christ**
- **Synthesis of the Upper Room and Gethsemane**
- **Synthesis of the Trial of Christ**
- **Synthesis of the Crucifixion**
- **Synthesis of the Resurrection Appearances**

# Notes

# Figure 18

## Synthesis of the Birth & Infancy of Christ

| Time Frame | Event | Matthew | Mark | Luke | John |
|---|---|---|---|---|---|
| From Eternity Into Time | The Incarnation of Jesus Christ. | | | | 1:1-18 |
| 9 Months | The Virgin Conception of Christ by the Holy Spirit and pregnancy. Joseph comes to terms by the Angel of the Lord's counsel and though not physically with her, he proceeds with the marriage. Mary visits Elizabeth. | 1:18-25 | | 1:26-56 | |
| Last Days of Pregnancy | Mary and Joseph travel to Bethlehem for taxation census. | | | 2:1-5 | |
| The Day of Birth | The Virgin Birth of Christ. | 1:25 | | 2:6-7 | |
| Later That Evening | The Shepherds are visited by the Angel of the Lord. | | | 2:8-12 | |
| Same Time | The Heavenly host praise God. | | | 2:13-14 | |
| After the Angelic Visit | The Shepherds go and visit the Baby Jesus. | | | 2:15-20 | |
| 8 Days Later | Baby Jesus circumcised. | | | 2:21 | |
| 33 Days Later (41 Since Birth) | After Mary's time of uncleanness, she goes to give the offering demanded in Leviticus 12:1-13 at the Temple in Jerusalem. (Jesus also presented as firstborn) | | | 2:22-24 | |
| While In Jerusalem | Simeon sees the Baby Jesus and rejoices. | | | 2:25-35 | |
| Still In Jerusalem | Anna praises God for the Baby Jesus. | | | 2:36-38 | |
| At End of Trip In Jerusalem | Mary and Joseph take Baby Jesus back to Bethlehem. | | | 2:39 | |

| Time Frame | Event | Matthew | Mark | Luke | John |
|---|---|---|---|---|---|
| **Somewhere Between 40 Days to the End of That Year** (*Daniel 9 Tells the Year*) | Wise Men travel from Babylon to Jerusalem. | 2:1 | | | |
| **Upon Arrival** | Wise Men meet Herod and wonder where the celebration is. They do not know to go to Bethlehem and have to ask. | 2:2-6 | | | |
| **After Meeting** | Herod sends Wise Men to Bethlehem asking them to return after meeting the King of the Jews. | 2:7-8 | | | |
| **On Journey of a Few Hours** (*8 Miles To Bethlehem*) | Star again leads Wise Men to Jesus. | 2:9-10 | | | |
| **Upon Arrival At Joseph and Mary's House In Bethlehem** | Wise Men worship Jesus and give gifts. | 2:11 | | | |
| **At End of Visit** | God warns the Wise Men to go another way and not to go to Herod and they obey. | 2:12 | | | |
| **After Wise Men Leave** | The Angel of the Lord tells Joseph to flee to Egypt. | 2:13 | | | |
| **That Same Night** | Joseph, Mary and Baby Jesus leave for Egypt. | 2:14-15 | | | |
| **After Herod Realized What Happened** | Herod has babies of Bethlehem killed - Jesus gone. | 2:16-18 | | | |
| **Probably 2 Years Since Birth** | Herod dies and the Angel of the Lord tells Joseph to go to Israel and he does. | 2:19-21 | | | |
| **On Journey Home** | Joseph is warned by God in a dream of Herod's son, Archelaeus, and he goes to Galilee where Jesus grows up. | 2:22-23 | | | |

## Figure 19

### Synthesis of the Upper Room and Gethsemane

| Location & Time Frame | Event | Matthew | Mark | Luke | John |
|---|---|---|---|---|---|
| On Tuesday night in Jerusalem, or the beginning of Wednesday to the Jewish people, beginning a 24 hr. cycle which will end with Jesus being buried. | As it becomes dark, Jesus and the 12 enter the Upper Room and sit to eat and the meal begins. | 26:20 | 14:17 | 22:14-18 | 13:1 |
| During Supper | Jesus washes the Disciple's feet and teaches on being a servant. | | | | 13:2-17 |
| | Jesus warns of a Betrayer and all ask "Is it I?" Jesus reveals that it is Judas but others do not notice. Judas leaves. | 26:21-25 | 14:18-21 | 22:21-23 | 13:18-30 |
| | Institution of the Lord's Supper. | 26:26-29 | 14:22-25 | 22:19-20 | |
| | Disciples argue over who is the greatest. Perhaps this is why they never noticed Judas as their minds were on this unspiritual subject. | | | 22:24-30 | |
| | Jesus speaks on Himself being glorified and reminds them of the commandment to love others. | | | | 13:31-35 |
| | Peter asks where Jesus is going and claims he will die with Christ. Christ gives first mention of Peter's denial. Jesus explains He is the need of their lives, but they ask about swords. | | | 22:31-38 | 13:36-38 |
| | Jesus gives His Comfort Discourse | | | | 14:1-31 |

| Time | Event | Matthew | Mark | Luke | John |
|---|---|---|---|---|---|
| As they walk from the Upper Room to Gethsemane | They leave the Upper Room. | 26:30 | 14:26 | 22:39 | 14:31b |
| | Jesus elaborates on all of them being offended because of Him that night and they all, and especially Peter, say it wasn't true. Jesus repeats His warning to Peter of his coming denial. | 26:31-35 | 14:27-31 | | |
| | Jesus gives His Vine and Branches Discourse. | | | | 15:1-16:33 |
| | Jesus stops before they cross the Brook Cedron and prays His High Priestly Prayer. | | | | 17:1-26 |
| As they enter the Garden of Gethsemane | They go into Gethsemane and He tells them to sit while He goes to pray taking Peter, James and John nearer His private place of prayer. | 26:36-37 | 14:32-33 | 22:40a | 18:1 |
| | Jesus enters His terror. He warns Peter, James and John to watch and pray. Three times He goes to pray; even collapsing, and 3 times He returns to find them sleeping. His agonies are beyond description as He sweats drops of blood. | 26:38-46 | 14:34-42 | 22:40b-46 | |
| | Judas arrives with a mob to arrest Jesus and betrays Him with a kiss. Jesus miraculously proclaims Himself the "I AM" and they all fall backward. | 26:47-50 | 14:43-45 | 22:47-48 | 18:2-9 |
| | Peter takes a sword and cuts off Malchus' ear. Jesus scolds him and miraculously heals the ear. | 26:51-54 | 14:46-47 | 22:49-51 | 18:10-11 |
| | Jesus is arrested and the Disciples scatter. | 26:55-56 | 14:48-50 | 22:52-53 | 18:12 |
| Sometime in the night as they leave Gethsemane | The mob leads Jesus away from Gethsemane and toward Caiaphas' house. | 26:57 | 14:51-53 | 22:54 | 18:13 |

# Figure 20

## Synthesis of the Trial of Christ and Corresponding Events

| Location & Time Frame | Event | Matthew | Mark | Luke | John |
|---|---|---|---|---|---|
| Sometime during Tuesday night (Wednesday in Jewish reckoning) as the mob led Jesus from Gethsemane | The mob grabs the linen cloth off of a young follower who runs off naked. Peter follows afar off, discouraged "to see the end." **The Convoy To Trial** | 26:57-58 a | 14:51-52 | 22:54 | |
| Inside the city of Jerusalem at Annas' House | Jesus is taken to Annas, the former High Priest and father-in-law to the current High Priest Caiaphas. During this time Peter begins his denials. **First Trial - Before Annas** | | | | 18:13-23 |
| Still at night and still in Jerusalem, Jesus is moved a short distance to Caiaphas' house | The Sanhedrin convenes and tries Jesus. False charges and false witnesses are used as well as illegal abuse. Peter continues his denials until he denied three times. When he and Christ made eye contact he left weeping bitterly. **Second Trial - Before Sanhedrin** | 26: 58b - 75 | 14:53-72 | 22:55-65 | 18:24-27 |
| At daybreak on Wednesday still at Caiphas' house in Jerusalem | The Sanhedrin reconvenes to get around the illegal night trial with results similar to the earlier one. Jesus is convicted. **Third Trial - Before Sanhedrin Again** | | | 22:66-71 | |
| Still early on Wednesday morning, taken to the Hall of Judgment slightly north of the Temple in Jerusalem | Jesus faces Pilate. The chief priests bring charges against Jesus with the charge being changed to rebellion against Caesar since He claims to be King of the Jews. Pilate admits, "I find no fault in him." At this time Judas commits suicide. **Fourth Trial - Before Pilate** | 27:1-14 | 15:1-5 | 23:1-5 | 18:28-38 |
| Another location in Jerusalem | Jesus faces Herod. Herod makes a mockery of the whole proceeding. Still, this helped relations between Pilate and Herod. **Fifth Trial - Before Herod** | | | 23:6-12 | |
| Back at the Hall of Judgment in Jerusalem | In this trial Pilate offers the release of a prisoner - Christ or Barabbas. His wife warns him against judging Jesus. He tries to get Jesus released but fears the Jews. Jesus would not try to help Pilate in securing His release. First putting on of crown of thorns and first scourging at this time. **Sixth Trial - Before Pilate Again** | 27:15-23 | 15:6-14 | 23:13-23 | 18:39-19:15 |
| | Jesus is sentenced to death. Pilate tries to put the blame on the Jews. Jesus is scourged again, stripped, and is arrayed in a scarlet robe. They put a crown of thorns back upon his head. **The Sentence - Guilty** | 27:24-30 | 15:15-20 | 23:24-25 | 19:16 |
| Moving north outside the gates of the city to Calvary arriving just before 9 a.m. | Jesus is taken to Calvary, the place of His execution. He bears His cross until Simon the Cyrenian is compelled to bear it for Him. Two thieves are taken at the same time and He tells some weeping women, "Weep not for me." **The Punishment - Crucifixion** | 27:31-34 | 15:21-22 | 23:26-32 | 19: 17 |

# Notes

# Figure 21

## SYNTHESIS OF THE DAY OF CRUCIFIXION

| TIME | EVENT | MATTHEW | MARK | LUKE | JOHN |
|---|---|---|---|---|---|
| 12:00 AM - 6:15 AM Dawn *(estimate)* | Midnight finds Christ somewhere in His illegal night trials. At the end, Jesus was held till daylight. | 26:57-68 | 14:53-65 | 22:54-65 | 18:12-27 |
| 6:15 AM - 9:00 AM | Last of religious trials before Sanhedrin. | | | 22:66-71 | |
| | **Begins Civil Trial: Part 1** *Before Pilate* | 27:2, 11-14 | 15:1-5 | 23:1-5 | 18:28-38 |
| | **Civil Trial: Part 2** *Before Herod* | | | 23:6-12 | |
| | **Civil Trial: Part 3** *Before Pilate again.* | 27:15-30 | 15:6-20 | 23:13-25 | 18:39-19:16 |
| | Scourged and mocked with crown of thorns and purple robe during this trial. | | | | |
| | Christ is led to Calvary (Golgotha). He bears His cross till Simon the Cyrenian is forced to bear it for Him to Golgotha. Tells women to "weep not". | 27:31-34 | 15:21-22 | 23:26-32 | 19:17 |
| 9:00 AM - 12:00 PM | **CRUCIFIXION** Begins as He is joined by two thieves and offered vinegar mingled with gall (a narcotic to deaden pain). He refuses to take it so He can drink all the bitter cup for us. (Nailed to the cross, sign over head and gambling for His garment) | 27:35-38 | 15:23-28 | 23:33-38 | 19:18-24 |
| | During this time He gives **1st cry** - *"Father, forgive them; for they know not what they do".* | | | 23:34 | |
| | Intense mocking and insults by crowd and even the two thieves. | 27:39-44 | 15:29-32 | | |
| | One thief turns to Christ and is saved **2nd cry** - *"Verily I say unto thee, To day shalt thou be with me in paradise".* | | | 23:39-43 | |
| | Jesus commits the care of Mary-his mother - to John **3rd cry** - *"Woman, behold thy son! Behold thy mother!"* | | | | 19:25-27 |
| 12:00 PM - 2:55 PM *(estimate)* | **DARKNESS COMES** *(silence)* | 27:45 | 15:33 | 23:44-45 | |
| 2:55 PM - 3:00 PM *(estimate)* | **LAST MOMENTS** 1. Out of the darkness Christ gives **4th cry** - *"My God, my God, why hast thou forsaken me?"* | 27:46-47 | 15:34-35 | | |
| | 2. Christ gives **5th cry** - *"I thirst"* and one runs over and puts vinegar to His lips which briefly strengthens Him. | 27:48-49 | 15:36 | | 19:28-29 |
| | 3. With strength to speak, Christ gives **6th cry** - *"It is finished."* | | | | 19:30a |
| | 4. Followed by **7th cry** - *"Father, into thy hands I commend my spirit."* | | | 23:46a | |

| TIME | EVENT | MATTHEW | MARK | LUKE | JOHN |
|---|---|---|---|---|---|
| 3:00 PM | **DEATH AND SIMULTANEOUS EVENTS**<br>1. Christ Jesus dies of His own will. | 27:50 | 15:37 | 23:46b | 19:30b |
| | 2. Rending of Temple veil (we have access to the Holy of Holies now). | 27:51a | | | |
| | 3. Earthquake. | 27:51b | 15:38 | | |
| | 4. Graves of many saints opened (they do not appear till resurrection). | 27:52-53 | | | |
| 3:01 PM - 6 PM<br>(estimate) | Light returns and amazed Roman soldier says "Truly this was the Son of God" as the women watched. | 27:54-56 | 15:39-41 | 23:47-49 | |
| | Jews ask to break their bones so crucifixion could be over by dusk when the high Sabbath of Passover begins. They find that Jesus is already dead. They pierce His side and blood and water pour out. | | | | 19:31-37 |
| | **THE BURIAL**<br>Joseph of Arimathaea and Nicodemus go to Pilate to beg for Jesus' body. | 27:57-58 | 15:42-45 | 23:50-52 | 19:38-39 |
| | Jesus' body is prepared for burial. | 27:59 | 15:46a | 23:53a | 19:40 |
| | Body is buried as the women watch before dusk | 27:60-61 | 15:46b-47 | 23:53b-55 | 19:41-42 |
| 7:00 PM<br>Dusk (estimate) | At some point all leave and three days begin.<br>At home the women prepare more spices. | | | 23:56 | |

COPYRIGHT 2010 BY James Reagan

# Figure 22

## Synthesis of the Events from the Resurrection to the Ascension

| Location & Time Frame | Event | Matthew | Mark | Luke | John |
|---|---|---|---|---|---|
| **EARLY SUNDAY MORNING BEFORE SUNRISE IN JERUSALEM** (JESUS ALREADY RISEN THOUGH THE EVENT IS NEITHER DESCRIBED NOR WITNESSED) | Mary Magdalene is part of a group of women coming to anoint Jesus' body and she arrives before the others and finds the stone rolled away. She runs to tell the others and meets Peter and John and tells of the rolled away stone and that Jesus' body is missing. | | | | 20:1-2 |
| | Peter and John go to the tomb and enter. They see the napkin that had been wrapped around His head neatly folded and the linen clothes there. They go home not comprehending it. | | | | 20:3-10 |
| | Mary stays weeping near the empty tomb. She sees two angels in the tomb who asks her why she weeps and she responds that it's because Jesus' body is taken away. She turns around and sees Jesus. **(1st Resurrection Appearance)** She doesn't realize it is Him as it is still dark and He speaks her name and then she knows it's her Lord. She isn't allowed to touch Him. | | | | 20:11-17a |
| | Jesus leaves and goes to Heaven as the High Priest and sprinkles the blood on the Mercy Seat of Heaven. Mary leaves. | | | | 20:17b-18 |
| **AT SUNRISE** *(TOLD IN FLASHBACK)* | The other women come to anoint Jesus' body and find the empty tomb. (We learn of an earlier earthquake and the guards fleeing as the stone rolled away) | 28:1 (28:2-4) | 16:1-4 | 24:1-3 | |
| | One angel sat on the rolled away stone but was apparently unnoticed. When inside the tomb there is again an angel at the head and feet of the empty grave and one angel proclaiming the fact of the Resurrection. He tells the women to go tell the disciples and the women leave. At some point, Mary Magdalene rejoins the group of women. | 28:5-8 | 16:5-8 | 24:4-8 | |
| | While going to tell the disciples, Jesus meets the group of women. **(2nd Appearance)** Now they touch Him and worship at His feet. He tells them to go on to the disciples. | 28:9-10 | | | |
| **AT THE SAME TIME THE WOMEN GO TO TELL THE DISCIPLES** | Guards go to the chief priests and accept a bribe. | 28:11-15 | | | |

| LOCATION & TIME FRAME | EVENT | MATTHEW | MARK | LUKE | JOHN |
|---|---|---|---|---|---|
| STILL EARLY ON SUNDAY | The women go and tell the disciples with Mary Magdalena especially appealing to them. The disciples didn't believe, but Peter returned to the empty tomb a second time in confusion. We later learn that Peter actually saw the Lord here (Luke 24:34) **(3rd Appearance)** | | 16:9-11 | 24:9-12 | |
| LATE THAT SUNDAY AFTERNOON | Jesus meets two on Emmaus Road, Cleopas and another. They were discouraged and Jesus talks with and encourages them but they didn't recognize Him. He explains their slowness in believing. As they neared the city they asked Him to stay and He had a meal with them and then vanished. **(4th Appearance)** | | 16:12-13 | 24:13-35 | |
| SUNDAY EVENING | Ten of the remaining eleven disciples were gathered in the secret Upper Room and Jesus appeared. He spoke of unbelief, but also of peace. He gives them the Holy Spirit. They handle him. **(5th Appearance)** | | | 24:36-43 | 20:19-25 |
| EIGHT DAYS LATER | All eleven are in the Upper Room and Jesus returns and meets with them. Thomas finally gets to see Jesus. Jesus also said and did things with those men that was not recorded. **(6th Appearance)** | | | | 20:26-31 |
| BETWEEN EIGHT AND FORTY DAYS FROM THE RESURRECTION ON THE SHORE OF GALILEE | The disciples are in the Galilee area because of the planned meeting. (Matthew 28:10) In discouragement Peter, John, and four other of the disciples fished all night and caught nothing. Jesus performed the miracle of the second drought of fishes and as the disciples drag in the fish Jesus has fish cooking on the fire. Jesus lovingly calls them back to their work. **(7th Appearance)** | | | | 21:1-25 |
| LATER STILL BETWEEN EIGHT AND FORTY DAYS FOR THE RESURRECTION IN GALILEE | Jesus meets the disciples and many other followers on a mountain in Galilee (probably the 500 - 1 Cor. 15:6). Here He gives the Great Commission. This is the only planned appearance. **(8th Appearance)** | 28:16-20 | | | |
| LATER STILL AS THE END OF FORTY DAYS DREW NIGH PROBABLY NEAR JERUSALEM (MAYBE EVEN BACK AT UPPER ROOM) | Jesus speaks to the eleven again and teaches them and repeats the Great Commission. Apparently speaking first with James. (1 Cor.15:7) **(9th Appearance)** | | 16:14-18 | 24:44-49 | |
| AT THE END OF FORTY DAYS ON A MOUNTAIN NEAR BETHANY JUST OUTSIDE JERUSALEM | The Ascension of Jesus Christ. The Incarnation ends and Jesus re-enters Eternity from which He came. **(10th Appearance)** | | 16:19-20 | 24:50-53 | |

## Conclusion

There is nothing in human history that compares to God the Son becoming flesh and living among us. His earthly sojourn made sense of all that happened before it, trumped all that happened during it, and defines the future after it. Every human being, to the good or the bad, must face what Christ accomplished while He walked this Earth. For those who embrace it, life is changed. The heart is changed. Eternity is changed.

What could be more important for a Bible student to learn than His earthly ministry as recorded in the Gospels? We do not need an academic prowess in regards to the Gospels, but a real understanding so that we may admire and learn. The Gospels are, perhaps, the greatest vantage point in this life from which to gaze upon Him Who our hearts love and adore. Let's not miss the chance.

www.ingramcontent.com/pod-product-compliance
Lightning Source LLC
LaVergne TN
LVHW012337290125
802515LV00008B/371